DATE DUE

DEMCO 38-296

THE
BRONSKI HOUSE

THE
BRONSKI HOUSE
A JOURNEY BACK

PHILIP MARSDEN

ARCADE PUBLISHING
NEW YORK

First U.S. Edition 1997

First published in Great Britain in 1995 by HarperCollins*Publishers*

ISBN 1-55970-392-X
Library of Congress Catalog Card Number 97–71364
Library of Congress Cataloging-in-Publication information is available.

Published in the United States by Arcade Publishing, Inc., New York
Distributed by Little, Brown and Company

10 9 8 7 6 5 4 3 2 1

PRINTED IN THE UNITED STATES OF AMERICA

CONTENTS

GLOSSARY

Bryczka *(Pol.)* – A small carriage
Czapka *(Pol.)* – A peasant cap
Chata *(Pol.)* – A hut or cabin
Dvornik *(Russ.)* – Yard-keeper
Dwór *(Pol.)* – A manor house
Dwórek *(Pol.)* – A small manor house
Graf *(Russ.)* – Count
Grafini *(Russ.)* – Countess
Hrabia *(Pol.)* – Count
Hrabina *(Pol.)* – Countess
Kresy *(Pol.)* – The lands of Eastern Poland
Kolkhoz *(Russ.)* – A collective farm
Kwas *(Pol.)* – Rye-beer
Pan *(Pol.)* – Mister
Pani *(Pol.)* – Mrs
Panna *(Pol.)* – Miss
Parobcy *(Pol.)* – Estate workers
Puszcza *(Pol.)* – Large natural forest
Sovkhoz *(Russ.)* – Large collective farm
Spiritus *(Russ.)* – Raw spirit, the base for vodka
Szlachta *(Pol.)* – Polish gentry
Tachanka *(Russ.)* – Springless cart
Wójt *(Pol.)* – Elected village head
Żubrówka *(Pol)* – A flavoured vodka

Author's Note

The names of the main families, as well as the names of the various estates, have been changed for the purpose of telling this story.

In Polish, first names have a series of diminutives and affectionate elaborations. 'Zofia' becomes 'Zosia' in familiar speech; likewise 'Helena' may become 'Hela' or 'Helutka' or 'Helenka'.

In the interest of simplicity, I have avoided using the vocative for reported speech; all names therefore appear in the nominative.

Poland's Shifting Borders 1914–1945

SWEDEN

Baltic Sea

E. PRUSS

GERMANY

R Elbe

●Posen

R Vist

R Odder

P

Cracow

SCALE

0   100   200 miles

Nie było nas
Był las.
Nie będzie nas
Będzie las.

(We were not here/ But the forest was./ We will not be here/
But the forest will be.)

Popular verse from Kresy, the borderlands of Eastern Poland

Mother Tongue wearing
a robe of mystical gold – liturgical – hieratic
(I see her always in gold, the Mother of Words)
Her pensive face, the gesture of hand absolving
this Prodigal Daughter who squandered, scattered
her heritage of words in foreign lands.

Zofia Ilińska

Zofia Ilińska's two volumes of poetry, *Horoscope of the Moon* and *Address of Paradise*, are published by Tabb House, 7 Church Street, Padstow, Cornwall.

PART I

ZOFIA

1

THERE WAS A HOUSE I knew as a child, grey-fronted, steep-lawned, with a bird's-eye view of a Cornish harbour. The house was set apart from the village, in its own ring of elm trees. From the lawn, you looked down the slope and over the treetops to a granite quay. The quay curled around the fishing tenders which bobbed about inside it. Beyond them, the bay widened towards a pair of headlands fringed with pine trees, a kind of gateway to the plains of the open sea.

In front of the house was a monkey-puzzle. It was tall and very straight with no branches until right at the top where a Medusa's-head of bracts burst out from the trunk. The tree had been planted by a sea-captain, one hundred and fifty years earlier. His last mission had been to take a member of the Portuguese royal family into exile in South America. For this he had been rewarded with a casket of gold and a bag of araucaria seeds. The gold he used to build the house. The seeds he planted in front of it. He called the house: Braganza.

For a few weeks every year we went to a cottage in the village below Braganza. It was August. The bay was hazy. White sails drifted across it. The chorus of the gulls was relentless. The lawn at Braganza, where we went to tea on Sundays, was as dry as a desert.

For years, Cornwall was the only abroad I knew. Crossing the Tamar, on an old stone bridge the colour of elephant skin, I closed my eyes and imagined it took two days; when I opened them again I felt sure we would be on some strange and far-off island. But it never worked. If Cornwall wasn't quite England, it wasn't quite abroad either.

I already knew what abroad would be like; it would be like

Braganza. There everything was different – the noises, the food, the smells. The voices you heard from the landing, from behind half-open doors, were foreign ones. Extraordinary things hung on the walls – wolfskins, bearskins, cutlasses, velvet-stocked muskets and icons. There were hand-tinted cartoons on the stairs, eerie wood-cuts of cobblers cobbling and reapers reaping, and perched on high marble plinths, looking somewhat like cockerels, was a vast array of silver samovars.

Braganza was a big house and there were parts of it I never saw. But I knew that some profound sadness lived in its more remote corners. Not an English sadness – a hushed thing, a 'don't-go-too-close-dear' sadness; this was a sadness without shame, something noble, a sadness that could face its own depths, a sadness rooted in truth – a sadness that was also the springboard for joy.

I did not know its name. But I sensed it had something to do with the framed photographs on a cabinet in the drawing room: the stern-gazed women, the tousle-haired sons with their rakish moustaches, the family groups picnicking in the forest. It probably had something to do with the painting of a long, low-fronted house and the larch tree which stood in front of it. But most of all it had to do with the woman who lived there.

Zofia was Polish. She spoke English in a spongy accent which she never lost. She called me 'Pheelip' and delivered her speech in such honeyed tones that sometimes listening to it, I would forget what she was saying and simply sit there watching her, letting the words fall over me like a balm. I loved her stories and her faraway looks, her pale translucent eyes. I loved the aura that surrounded her. I loved her sadness.

The year I was born Zofia had her fortieth birthday. Her husband owned the two harbourside hotels below the house. He staffed them with waiters from southern Italy who started fights and gave babies to the local girls. When I was five, Zofia bent down to me and whispered, 'Pheelip, will you be my friend, my special friend?'

'Yes, please!'

'I have four boyfriends already,' she confessed. 'My husband, my son and my two dogs. But you, Pheelip, you must be one too. Would you like that?'

After that not a Christmas went by without some surprise gift arriving in the post – an onyx egg, an old postcard of a place called Wilno, a Polish bank note, a pen. The pen was a magic one, she said – it will write magic things for you. She herself wrote magic things: witty, lyrical poems about amorous unicorns, talking lobsters and the strange gentlemen who stayed in her hotels.

Each August she took my brother and me to lunch in one of the hotels. We had to wear ties, and tweed jackets which were too big one year and too small the next. Zofia called the Italian waiters by name (usually the wrong one) and ordered complicated things like prawns and oysters which we slipped into our pockets when she wasn't looking. But afterwards she would concede to our tastes and ask for rice pudding, which she pronounced 'Rasputin'.

Then we went onto the terrace and she told stories – fabulous stories, Polish stories. The tide lapped at the wall below us; boats criss-crossed the bay. But Zofia would lean forward, her voice softened to a whisper, and conjure up a much more compelling picture of a darkened forest thick with snow, of howling wolves and a howling wind, of a man all alone in the corner of a clapboard cabin, listening, listening: 'Vooosh-vooosh! goes the wind . . . Awooo, awooo! go the wolves . . .'

Zofia made very convincing noises, and we were there in that clapboard cabin, there with that lonely man, with the whooshing wind, the awooing wolves – listening, listening, listening . . .

She would then thump the table and cry out and we would

all laugh – the two of us with shock, Zofia with mischief, while the starchy English guests at the next tables would raise their eyebrows at the unseemly way this woman – this foreign woman, the hotel's proprietress – behaved in public with her two little boys.

Zofia had a small boat called *Memory* with a 17 on the mainsail. Seventeen was the age she was when she escaped, and seventeen was the date: 17 September 1939.

She was the worst sailor I have ever known. Utterly unable to grasp the principle of the points of sail – the tacking, the going-about, the gybing – she reverted instead to techniques that she *did* understand: those for riding a horse. She treated the sheets like reins, the halyards like a throat-lash. Her dogs swam alongside and helped to convince her that sailing – feeling the breeze in her hair, contemplating the big questions – was really no different from a ride in the Polish forest.

The language of sailing baffled her too. Each time she rowed out to *Memory*, she first asked Jimmy Green in the boatyard for his advice: 'Oh, Jeemy, what is the tide doing?'

'Comin' in, Mrs Mo,' he'd say, or, 'Goin' out now.'

But by the time she'd reached *Memory*, she couldn't remember whether it was 'coming in' or 'coming out', or 'going in' or 'going out'. Nor was she quite sure why it mattered.

On occasions, after some near calamity, she would turn to old Charlie Ferris ('Whiskers' on account of his enormous white beard) and ask him, again, to try and teach her to sail. Whiskers would come aboard and point out the sheets and cleats, for'ard and aft, port and starboard, would show her how to find the wind and set the sails, and she'd pretend to understand. But one day she lost the main halyard up the mast and Whiskers, shinnying up to get it, forfeited a large chunk of his beard to a block. After that he wouldn't go near *Memory* again.

I was ten and a half when, one August evening, Zofia telephoned our cottage and asked for me.

'Pheelip,' she said, in a deep voice reserved for adventures, 'I am taking *Memory* up the creek to see the swans. Will you come?'

The oak trees came right down to the water. Seaweed hung like witches' hair from their boughs. Rounding the first bend, we found the ribs of an abandoned ship, but no swans. By the time we rounded the second bend, the evening had cast its spell on the deserted creek and Zofia purred, 'Oh, isn't it beautiful!'

And so it was. But the briny scum on the water, the floating twigs and eel grass, had already begun to ebb. Unnoticed they slipped past *Memory*'s hull, while what breeze there was nudged us upstream. Pretty soon there came a soft jolt and *Memory* was lodged firmly in the mud.

'Oh dear!' said Zofia.

There was no alternative but to drop the sails and wait for the flood. Zofia didn't mind a bit.

It became dark. The moon rose. The curlew cried from the mud flats. Zofia's dogs fell asleep on the bottom-boards. The night filled with little noises.

At first we were silent.

Then Zofia began to sing. She sang in a deep, modulated voice thick with Slavic irony. She sang a Belorussian song about a priest and his dead dog. She tried to teach it to me but I couldn't make the sounds. She then told a story about two lovers, a ferry on the river Niemen, and a murder; she asked me to decide who was to blame.

'The man?'

'Perhaps . . .'

'The woman?'

'Perhaps . . .'

'The ferryman?'

She laughed and her laughter echoed in the creek. Leaning back against the folds of the mainsail, she took each of the suspects in turn and explained how, in the real world, the grown-up world, everyone could be culpable – or no one. Looking up at the stars, she then sighed and recited a poem of hers in which the poet envies a scarecrow: 'I wish there was no thought in me / this head of thought exhausteth me.'

The hours slid past and she settled into a long lilting monologue, punctuated by the cries of the night birds, of the old life in Eastern Poland – the villages and wolf hunts, the larger-than-life people. Scene by scene fell on our marooned boat like the miraculous crystals of dew: funeral carriages in the snow, dead bodies in the river, the sad ghost who sat on her bed complaining, the dragoon who galloped along the river bank, naked but for his leather top-boots.

Then there was the escape itself – Russian tanks approaching through the forest, a hurried flight on farm-carts, the poison her mother carried in a small glass bottle, the final drama at the Lithuanian frontier with bullets screeching around their ears.

But of all the things that she told me that evening, it was the story of the silver that lodged most firmly in my boyish mind. Real treasure, not just the imagined treasure of a vanished world; real treasure, taken into the forest in mushroom baskets before the escape, buried deep in a new plantation, abandoned to hope, while the two most destructive armies the world had ever seen rumbled towards each other through the trees.

'Is it still there, Zosia?'

'Maybe.'

'Why don't you go and see?'

'They will not allow me.'

'But one day they will let you, won't they, Zosia?'

'Yes.'

2

THE YEARS PASSED and we no longer went to Cornwall. I broke free of a protracted education, moved to London, and Zofia and Poland slipped into that burgeoning slush-fund of half-forgotten places and half-forgotten people. I still received word from her – a meditation from Spain on the theme of 'hot sun and accidie', telephone calls in which she would demand to know if I was 'in lerff', and sprigs of thrift and sea-rocket in the post, lest she and Cornwall should ever slip too far from my thoughts.

Then came a call announcing a six-month trip to Australia: would I come and see her off?

'Of course,' I said.

'I leave on Sunday week. At noon.'

'From Heathrow?'

'No! From Tilbury.'

She had taken a berth on a Polish cargo ship. I carried her two suitcases up the gangplank. In one were her clothes (jerseys for the Bay of Biscay, cotton dresses for the tropics), in the other, books. She pushed open her cabin door and sat down on the bunk. Down the companionway came the shouts of the crew, Polish shouts, and Zofia looked at me sadly and smiled: it reminded her of home.

I left her on board. I watched the grey hull slide off down the Thames. I pictured her unpacking her books in the cabin and thought, for the first time, of what her exile really meant – that perpetual rootlessness, the ceaseless sense of un-belonging, the warding off of bitter thoughts. Over the coming months a series of fat envelopes fell through my door – post-marked Genoa, Alexandria, Dubai, and filled with Zofia's 'Poems of the Sea'. These confirmed it, helping to convince me that exile, long sea voyages, all that gradual dissipation of place, held in them some secret capacity for revelation.

The following year I wrote to Zofia saying I was leaving London. I was coming to live in Cornwall.

A letter came back by return. 'So,' she wrote, 'I'm afraid the Furies have finally got to you!' But she was delighted.

I arrived back in the village at dusk on a slow January day. It was blowing a gale. The seas were rising in sudden bomb-bursts above the quay wall, to flop down over the road and douse the boarded-up buildings. I unlocked the cottage, dumped my things, then went up the hill to see Zofia.

Braganza was unchanged – the photographs, the bearskins, the samovars. The monkey-puzzle stood unmoving in the gale. But a certain calm had settled on the house. The rooms echoed with absence. Where were the pasty-skinned men and their old-world suits, the Finnish cook, the summer hordes of French children? The old Polish cavalry officer and the painter from Cracow, the mysterious poet from Poznan?

Zofia was alone. She sat reading in a high-backed chair. She put down her book as I entered, and slipped off her glasses. 'Pheelip, how lovely to see you.'

She was now widowed. Her daughter was living in France, her son had been killed in a car crash. *Memory* had been sold to a judge. Several generations of dogs had come and gone. The ring of elm trees outside had gone too, gnawed to death by arboreal beetles. On her mantelpiece was a plywood banner reading: 'SOLIDARNOSC'; it was the time of martial law in Poland.

Yet none of these things had dented Zofia's spirit. She seemed unembittered, perennial, robust. Her speech retained those honeyed tones, her presence remained magnetic. Over the coming months, I found her still mischievous, still writing, still surrounded by that Slavic aura – and by her dogs, three of them, which slept like angels at her feet. If anything she seemed happier.

'Oh goodness, yes! It's much better to be seventy than your age.'

'Why?' I asked.

She leaned towards me. 'None of that confusion of sex!'

One afternoon I went up to Braganza and discovered Zofia kneeling on the floor, flanked by notebooks and files. 'My mother's papers,' she sighed, then started for the first time to tell me about her. She became animated; her Polish accent thickened. Her arms were raised at the dredging up of old grievances, dropped to her sides at the thought of what had been lost. She railed against the impossible demands her mother had made on occasions. 'Yet she was one of the most extraordinary people I have ever known.'

'In what way?'

Zofia paused. 'Almost every way. She could charm a hawk off a tree. Her conversation was brilliant. In her presence everything became uplifted, gayer. She was almost like a saint in some ways. But, my God, such things happened all around her!'

'What sort of things?'

Zofia turned towards me. She paused; the question was too big to answer. 'Wars . . . calamities . . . always fleeing . . .' Then she pushed the papers across the carpet. 'But it's all here! It's all in here. Why not read them?'

I took the papers to my cottage, the notebooks and letters and diaries, even some short stories. Many were in English; others Zofia had translated. For four days, a week, I read and re-read those papers. The shadowy world of Zofia's pre-war past came to life. The scenes she had conjured up for me years earlier were re-shaped, fleshed out, in hundreds of pages of her mother's pale blue script.

A damp, woody smell rose from the notebooks as I read them; passions and betrayals rose with them. Old Europe had been caught like a fly and squashed between those yellowing pages. Zofia's mother took hold of me.

She was born on 17 July 1898, at a house called Platków in the northern regions of Russian Poland. On the night of her birth a great storm swept through the forests, scattering the pines like matchsticks. For years afterwards, the trees lay where they had fallen and Zofia's mother assumed that devastation was the natural state of things.

They christened her Helena. On her mother's side she came from a traditional Polish land-owning family, with a traditional land-owning aversion to alien things. This was the world to which Helena was entitled, for which she was born, the one into which she should have settled quite comfortably but for two things. That world, as she always sensed, was coming to an end. And she had inherited a foreign name.

Her father was called O'Breifne. He was the direct descendant of Lochlainn, last king of East Breifne. Lochlainn had ruled lands just to the south of Ulster in the fifteenth century. But two hundred years later, with the kingdom gone, his heirs were forced to flee the English after the Battle of the Boyne and head for France.

From France the O'Breifnes went to Russia, three brothers invited by the Empress Elizabeth to train the Tartar wildness from her army officers. One of the brothers, Cornelius, the only one to have issue, settled there. Though his family remained in Russia, they were never naturalized. Cornelius's son became a famous general (his portrait hangs in St Petersburg's Gallery of Heroes). Tsar Alexander I was godfather to his children, but he could not bring himself to forfeit the one thing he retained from the old country: his faith.

'Never forget', his father had told him, 'that you are a Catholic and an Irishman.'

Obliged to become Orthodox if he married a Russian, his only option was to marry a Pole. Three generations followed suit. The Irish blood was diluted. Yet in the stifling climate of Eastern Poland's landed families, Helena and the O'Breifnes were always outsiders. They read books, for one thing. Some of them had liberal Tolstoyan ideas. They discussed dangerous things like land reform. And there was always that name.

The O'Breifnes, as Helena was reminded, constantly, by the stage whispers of dusty dowagers, were 'not really true Poles'.

Zofia too remembered the whispers. 'All these grand Polish women used to pretend they couldn't pronounce it. "Orbrefna? Orbrefska? What sort of a name is that? There's dozens of them in Ireland . . . Living in hovels all over the place . . ."'

On one visit to Braganza Zofia handed me an envelope. Out of the envelope fell two photographs. They were the only ones to have survived the war.

The first picture was taken on the edge of a forest in 1936. Helena was bending down, with one hand on the back of a dog. She was looking up at the camera and her mouth was set in a half smile. There was a kind of sprung vitality about her.

'That was taken near the house at Mantuski, with Barraj, one of the Great Danes.'

The other picture was a studio portrait, taken in Warsaw in 1919. Helena was almost twenty. I looked at her white high-collared dress, the cocked head, the smile and her narrow eyes, the strange polished complexion of her face.

Zofia pointed a finger at it. 'You see here the way she is toying with the necklace, below the neck? She used to say that that was the way to make a man fall in love with you.' Zofia hushed her voice. 'You know, I believe it works! I have even tried it a few times . . .'

I looked closely at the two pictures. I tried to tell myself it was something else. It was the diaries, the letters, her extraordinary story; it was the way that this woman, Helena O'Breifne, had crossed the steepest contours of our age; that for me, living in flatter decades, in a quieter corner of Europe, her world represented everything that had been lost, a place of slow villages, muddy livestock and unfenced fields, of time passing with only the backdrop of the seasons, of lives exaggerated – exaggerated in wealth, in poverty, in suffering – lives buffeted by a history no one seemed to control: Helena's was a bigger world, a crueller world, a world of half-mad nobles living on borrowed time, of noble peasants living outside time, another Europe, an older Europe.

But of course Zofia was right. My interest was also much more commonplace. It had just as much to do with the way Helena toyed with her necklace.

3

I WENT AWAY for six months and returned to Cornwall the following spring. At Braganza, Zofia was combing the hair of her dachshund. Out of the window, I could see daffodils at the foot of the monkey-puzzle. The bay beyond was grey-blue and ruffled. The SOLIDARNOSC banner had gone from the mantelpiece.

Zofia greeted me with her sad, open, blue-eyed smile.

'Pheelip, how good you're back!'

We sat and talked for a while, then her eyes lit up and she said, 'Look, I've got something to show you. Something extra-ordinary!'

She stood, and from the next room fetched a large marquetry jewel-box. Among the strings of pearls, the amber brooches, the diamanté ear-rings, was a wedge of concrete. 'It came last week in the post. Can you guess what it is?'

I shook my head.

'From Berlin! My cousin sent it.' She picked out the small relic and held it. 'The wall. It's a piece of the wall.'

She paused. Decades of loss crossed her face. I knew that expression well; her whole being seemed about to burst with the force of what was behind it: the half century of separation, her two lives torn apart, Europe torn in two.

It was fifty-two years since she had fled that morning, on a farm cart, in the early autumn of 1939. And since then, nothing. Not a word of news had reached her – of the village, or the house, or the people she had known. After Yalta the Poland she knew was no longer Poland. It was Stalin's Belorussia, and a part of it too close to the border to let foreigners visit. Not even rumours slipped out – only wild speculation: that the village had been destroyed in the war, turned into a military camp by the Soviet army, contaminated by fall-out from Chernobyl.

Zofia replaced the concrete fragment and closed the box. 'I am going back, Pheelip. I don't think I could die not knowing what happened. You will come with me?'

'Of course.'

'Maybe we will find the silver!'

'Maybe,' I said.

For a year or so I heard nothing and wondered whether, on reflection, Zofia had decided against lifting the lid on all those monsters from her old world. I went to the Middle East, to Egypt and Israel. One evening in the old town of Jaffa, a letter caught up with me:

> My dear Philip,
>
> You haven't forgotten our journey, have you? I was thinking of next May or June. I hope that suits you. How should we go about getting visas – does the Soviet Embassy still deal with Belorussia? Should we drive? Everyone says the place is full of bandits! I hope we'll be safe. It would be maddening to be slaughtered there after all these years.
>
> Torquil my dachshund is ill. The weather is lovely, the bay deep deep blue. Are you writing? I have started an enormous long poem about 'roots'.
>
> My love to you, dear Philip. Z.

Back in London, someone gave me the name of a Polish art dealer in Jermyn Street. He put me onto a professor in Minsk, who in turn issued an invitation. After a couple of mornings standing on the pavement outside the Soviet consulate, I had the visas. I took them down to Cornwall at the end of April. Zofia was working in her flowerbed.

'Oh, how marvellous, Pheelip! Look!' She slipped off her gloves, took the visas and thumbed through them. 'So, we are really going!'

Only the sight of her own name written in Cyrillic muted her enthusiasm.

We spent several days in preparation. I re-read Helena's papers; Zofia bought some crêpe-soled shoes. 'Travelling shoes,' she whispered. 'Ghost-hunting shoes!'

The day before our departure we walked to a creek above Ruan Lanihorne. It was the first week of May. The woods were covered in a tentative, filmy green; toadflax tumbled from an old stone bridge. The river bubbled beneath it, before sliding into the creek, losing itself in the tide.

'Duty,' mused Zofia. 'Perhaps more than anything else my mother drummed into me the notion of duty.'

'Is it your duty to go back?'

'No.' She shook her head. 'That's something else. I am going back for myself, not for my mother. No, it was more a code she had, a fiercely rigid code of duty that ordered her whole life.'

'And yet she was always trying to escape.'

'Yes, or being forced to.'

When Helena wasn't fleeing marauding armies, she seemed to be struggling perpetually against the strictures of her own position – her mother, her family, her suitors.

The earliest story in her diaries concerns a brief spell at a convent in Cracow. She was fourteen; the year was 1913. On arriving at the convent, she had looked at the other girls, at the nuns, at the shiny brown corridors; and for two weeks plotted her escape. One night she took a loaf of bread and a flask of water and climbed the convent wall.

It was a still, cold night and the frost was thick. Helena crouched on the wall, ready to jump.

'Helena O'Breifne! Stay where you are!'

She froze. It was the headmistress, standing beneath the wall.

'Helena!'

'Yes, Mother Immaculate.'

'What do you think you're doing?'

She said nothing.

'You'll never get anywhere without your passport. Here, I have it with me. If we hurry we can reach the station for the Warsaw train. What do you think?'

Helena's plan crumbled before her. It seemed suddenly childish and naive. She climbed back into the convent grounds.

Mother Immaculate took her inside and sat her in her office. 'Now, Hela, I know how unhappy you feel. But it would be a terrible waste if you didn't study. Don't you agree?'

Helena nodded.

'I want us to be friends. You must come and see me whenever you want.'

How can one be friends with a nun? thought Helena. But over the coming weeks, she found herself spending more and more time with Mother Immaculate. They sat in her office and talked after Mass. The other girls chastised Helena for it, but she didn't mind. For the first time she felt affection for someone who was not one of her family – nor one of her animals. No one else, before or since, encouraged her in quite the same way.

The following summer, during the holidays, Mother Immaculate wrote to say she was passing through Wilno. Could she come and see the O'Breifnes? Helena was delighted. 'Look, Mama, you will meet Mother Immaculate!'

Her mother read the letter. She shook her head. 'Your friendship with this nun is not natural. I forbid you to see her.'

That autumn Mother Immaculate was posted to China. She was sent to teach in an Ursuline mission. Though Helena wrote to her frequently, and received long letters in reply, and though in these letters she gained constant reminders of the duty she had to her own talents, and though the phrases in those letters stayed with her for the rest of her life, she never saw Mother Immaculate again.

In 1916 this elderly nun was attacked on the steps of her own chapel by the lackeys of a Chinese warlord. Helena received news of her death early in 1917.

The tide had crept up the creek. A cold wind was blowing from the north. Zofia pulled up her collar and said, 'Yes, I remember that story. She had those letters at Mantuski. She kept them in a Chinese ivory box. Goodness knows what became of them. Looted I suppose, like everything else . . .'

She looked up into the trees. The boughs of the scrub-oak were twisted into strange, serpentine forms. 'What are we going to find, Pheelip? What will we find there?'

4

ON A DAMP MAY NIGHT, we crossed the border into
Belorussia. The train pulled into a siding to be raised on vast
hydraulic jacks – Polish bogies rolled out, Soviet bogies rolled
in. Border guards climbed on board to inspect papers; the 'jer-
jink' of their stamps rang out along the corridor.

Inside the old Soviet Union, I opened a bottle of vodka.
We toasted the crossing and Zofia tapped the bottle and said,
'Pheelip, I think we might need this again. Will you keep it
to hand?'

We reached Minsk at about two a.m. The train pitched us
out onto a dark platform, then sped on into the night, on
towards Moscow. Zofia shivered. She looked at the dim ranks
of Soviet buildings, the alien shapes of Cyrillic script and said,
'Ach! What a grim place!'

Her fear of Russia was something elemental, instinctive. It
had been bred into her with the unassailable prejudices of frontier peoples. She had been brought up in the shadow of the
new Soviet border, less than sixty miles to the east of Mantuski.
In those days, only stories permeated its barbed-wire coils,
stories and bodies floating face-down in the waters of the
Niemen. She learnt two things intuitively: that upstream in
Russia, they killed girls like her, nice land-owning girls; and
that peril, when it came, came always from the east.

'Do you know that the first Russians I ever saw were the
soldiers in the trees as we fled into Lithuania.'

And here she was, at two in the morning, fifty years later,
east of her old home, on Soviet soil for the first time.

A war-like darkness hung over the city. I found a taxi which crept through the lampless streets in search of a hotel. At the first one, they said, 'Nyet!' At the second the receptionist didn't even bother saying 'Nyet!' but simply shook her head. At the third they said, 'Nyet!' and the taxi driver came to argue. They still said, 'Nyet.'

He and I stepped out again onto the street. In our absence, a man had got into the car. I could see Zofia cowering in the back. I ran across just as he jumped out, slipped around the other side, beat the car's roof, then started to flap his arms like a bird. Before we could stop him, he was off, shouting bestially.

I opened the car door. Zofia was laughing, but in the darkness I could see her hands clasped tight over her handbag. They were shaking.

'Oh, Pheelip, thank God you came back! Was he mad, do you think, or just drunk?'

Either way, it confirmed her worst prejudices.

We returned to the first hotel and, in the end, managed to bully a couple of rooms from them. The hotel in fact was virtually empty. In a room on the eighth floor, I reopened the vodka and poured two glasses.

'Well, Zosia,' I said. 'To success!'

'Success,' she said, unconvincingly.

'Are you afraid?'

She looked up at me and nodded.

'Of what?'

'I don't know, Pheelip. I just feel a deep apprehension. Perhaps this is all madness. I mean, how can we go back? How can we ever go back?'

I tried to see it through her eyes. How could I? Reading Helena's diaries had only made me realize how distant it all was, how completely 1939 had divided their lives into two.

She looked down, fingering her watch-strap. 'I don't know, I just don't know . . .'

When she looked up again, she said, 'You remember what Konrad Lorenz said about those rats, how if one is killed they mark the place with their urine? Then the others know not to go back . . . and here am I – going back! It is madness!' She raised her glass. 'More vodka, Pheelip! Then I am going to bed.'

I stumbled back down the ill-lit corridor. I could not sleep. I propped the bottle on the window-sill of my room and looked out. The city of Minsk winked lamely in the night. This trampled, luckless city! Twice destroyed – once in the first war, again in the second. Eighty per cent of Belorussia's towns and villages had been destroyed in the second war; one in four of its people had died. Zofia was seventeen that time; Helena was seventeen the first time.

I kept thinking of the patterns their two lives made across this dark century. Helena came of age with it, lost her innocence with it, was there – in St Petersburg, in 1917 – at the outset of its great and glorious experiment, the same experiment which forced her, several times, to flee for her life. Zofia and the new-bordered Poland were born in the same year, Polish twins, and both were seventeen when the borders collapsed: seventeen, 1917, 17 September, 17 on *Memory*'s distant, flapping mainsail.

Czesław Miłosz was born ten years before Zofia, in the same town, Wilno. '1914', he once wrote, 'was the manifestation of all of Europe's defects and of her end . . . the longed-for war of nations had brought Poland to life as a posthumous creation.'

Looking over the dark, lifeless pathways of modern Minsk, thinking of Helena when young, Zofia when young, the Russia of Turgenev and Tolstoy, the Poland of Mickiewicz and Reymont, I found the idea a compelling one: of living in a posthumous Europe, a Europe repeating in death precisely the mistakes it had made in life.

*   *   *

The next morning was bright; from my window, I could see the early mist lingering over the municipal lakes. In the hotel café Zofia was already up, already surrounded by coffee and books and bread, and already talking to a man called Vladimir. Vladimir was an enormous man. He had thick black hair and hairy bear hands. His story as he told it began in 1940 when a Polish girl, a frail Polish village girl, first held in her arms the little bundle that was to become Vladimir. His father, she told him, had been a Russian officer. The war had brought him to the village, and the war had taken him away. For years Vladimir wondered about this man, this ghost of a man who was his father. When doing his national service he began his search: it went on for fifteen years. 'Fifteen yerrs lukeing!'

In Moscow he had some success. He tracked down another of this man's children. It seemed that Vladimir had twelve half-brothers scattered across the Union. Through a series of letters they all agreed to meet in Moscow.

'Well, when I see them,' explained Vladimir, 'when I see them on railway station I hug, hug, hug. Twelve times hug! An the teers they come up, they roll like peas down the cheek. Like grreat beeg peas!'

Afterwards, when Vladimir had taken his briefcase off into the new uncertainties of the morning, Zofia tutted, 'My goodness, how they weep, these poor people!'

Later I found her bending over a book in her room; she too had been weeping.

'The dogs . . . You know, we abandoned them when we escaped, we left them behind . . .'

She was reading the account of a wounded partisan in a cave in 1940. A skeletal creature appeared at the cave mouth, licked the partisan's face, then curled up at his side, dead.

'Perhaps that was one of ours . . .'

And the tears rolled down her cheeks like peas.

*　　*　　*

We left Minsk a couple of days later, on a road lined with wooden cabins painted blue and green and yellow. Our contacts had found a Lada and a Russian driver named Andrei. We drove west, beyond the fringes of the city, into the forest. A muddy sky hung over the morning, swollen with rain. Beneath it the land had flattened itself, and cowered in the shadows. We drove in silence. The forest thickened, the villages became fewer, then gave way altogether to the Puszcza Nalibocka, an expanse of bison-filled, tree-covered territory the size of a small county. The rain began to fall in large droplets which shattered on the windscreen. Andrei stopped the car, jumped out, clenched his lapels together and with his other hand attached the wiper-blades.

The cloud dropped. It wrapped itself around the pine-tops. In places there were clearings, but beyond them more trees, more forest. It gave the impression of some grim eternity.

Zofia sighed. She was looking out of the window, watching the trees slip past. I could sense her turmoil, could see in her eyes a shadow of the old catastrophe. We did not speak.

The *puszcza* ended and the trees gave way to fields. Cattle dotted the damp green spaces and then suddenly the clouds were broken and the sun was shining. It shone on the meadows and farm tracks, on the steaming thatched roofs of hay barns. The Niemen was now quite close. Mantuski was less than an hour away.

Zofia turned to me and smiled, whispering, 'Pheelip, do you know I can hardly believe it! Before the sun sets I will be in Mantuski, after fifty-three years – and I am being driven there by a Russian who seems in no way intent on killing me!'

Leaving the main road, we drove down a barely metalled track towards Mantuski village. There was one long street and two rows of wooden cabins. Flashing between the buildings was the pale fish-back blue of the river Niemen.

We pulled up beside the village well. An old man was sauntering up the road, in and out of the shade of the chestnuts. The sun was low behind the trees.

The old man reached us. He looked up at us each in turn, his head askew. Zofia shook his hand and said to him, 'I am Panna Brońska. Zofia Brońska.'

The old man blinked. 'What?'

'I am Zofia Brońska.'

'Zofia Brońska?'

'Yes.'

He took off his cap, blinked again. He looked up at her and frowned. 'Little Zośka?'

She nodded.

'*Nie . . . nie prawda . . . nie prawda*, little Zośka on a pony! In a red dress with your hair in plaits by the river . . . Panna Zośka, Panna Zośka, *nie prawda, nie prawda* . . .'

Then the tears overtook him and he could not speak.

Zofia bent and kissed the old man and she too was weeping.

'. . . my pony, yes, you remember, and the red dress . . .'

The old man pulled away from her again. He looked up at her with flooded eyes. 'But why,' he spluttered, 'why you are so old?'

I asked him about the house.

'The house? The *dwór*?' the old man was struggling to light a cigarette. 'Nie ma!' he inhaled sharply. 'Nie ma domu.'

So that was it: *nie ma domu*. No house. I looked at Zofia; she seemed too dazed to register it.

'Let's go and look anyway,' I said.

We drove on, through the village, beyond the last houses. Zofia was watching carefully.

'It was some way beyond the village . . . these cabins are new . . . there was a cross, Michał's Cross we called it, I don't remember where exactly . . . and then the avenue. But none of this I recognize . . .'

We re-entered the forest. The Niemen was off to the left, through the trees. We carried on, slowly, and the forest gave way to a wide field of potatoes.

'No, this must be too far.'

We cut down through the trees to the river, and back along the bank.

'Oh, the Niemen . . . look at it . . .' Zofia watched its spinning, turbulent flow. 'Perhaps there is just nothing left of the house, nothing at all . . .'

I felt angry at her nonchalance, the old villager's nonchalance. 'There must be something!' I said. 'Are you sure that none of this you recognize?'

'Vaguely . . . the river . . .'

'What about those buildings?' Ahead were some low farm buildings.

'Vaguely . . .'

But I saw they were new. Maybe she was right. And maybe it didn't matter. Perhaps it was simply literal-mindedness on my part to feel the need, if not for the walls and roof, at least for some ruins, for a corpse.

'Wait.' Zofia sat forward. 'There, that must have been the brick factory. So the house was in there somewhere.'

We drove through a *kolkhoz* yard. Two poplars rose above a well.

'No, no, this isn't right.' Zofia sat back. 'It's all changed.'

Beyond the *kolkhoz*, the horizon was broken by a tall and scruffy tree. In Helena's diaries, there'd been a larch on the lawn in front of the house.

'That larch, Zosia. What do you think?'

She leaned forward again. 'I think you may be right – yes . . . yes, that's it!'

We got out of the car and walked, down a grassy path and through an orchard. The larch stood on a low mound.

'That's the larch!'

'So where's the house?'

'There!'

I followed her gaze: a few bushes, some hazel trees, and beneath them, the stunted, grassed-over remains of some walls. That was all.

Zofia put a hand to her cheek. 'Oh my goodness! The poor house has crawled away!'

She stepped onto the ruins. She took a small plastic bag from her pocket and filled it with soil. 'To sprinkle on my coffin,' she explained and suddenly she was grinning at herself, at the trees, at the absurdity of it all, at the baffling distance between her two lives.

5

WE STAYED IN the small town of Iwje that night. The next morning was bright and warm. We went back to Mantuski early. As we walked down the street, Zofia looked at the bright yellow-painted cabins, and said, 'Oh, thank God I came! What marvellous days these are!'

Behind us there was the click of a gate. 'Proszę Pani! Pani Zośka!'

The old man from the day before hobbled up to us. 'Proszę Pani, I'm sorry. I'm sorry for yesterday.'

'It doesn't matter. Honestly.'

'Only I was drunk. I meant to give you this, you see. I've been keeping it.' He held out an old silver knife. It was broken. 'From the dwór, Pani Zośka. I found it at the dwór. And I kept it for you.'

She smiled. 'Please, keep it.'

He pointed down the road. 'There's Pani Wala wanting to see you down there beyond the school.'

'Pani Wala – the seamstress?'

The old man nodded. 'Beyond the school!'

We carried on.

'Yes, I remember Wala,' said Zofia. She had been descended from a foundling. Her grandmother had been abandoned and taken in by Zofia's grandmother.

We found her house. Bantam chicks scurried out of her yard. I knocked on the door. An old woman appeared in a sunflower housecoat. She saw Zofia, and burst into tears.

Zofia took her hand and they sat on a bench in the sun.

Pani Wala could not believe it. 'Pani Zofia . . . this is a vision, I am seeing a vision . . .'

Zofia talked with her for a minute or two, then asked about the house.

'. . . Yes, they burnt the house, they took off its clothes and burnt it.'

'Who?' asked Zofia.

She shook her head. She was overcome. She looked at Zofia and rolled her head from side to side. 'Oj-oj-oj Pani Zofia, it is like a dream your coming . . . so many things have happened so many deaths so many births . . . mountain cannot meet mountain but man will meet man again . . .'

Zofia repeated her question about the house.

'Partisans, it was the partisans . . .'

Partisans. Every story here led back to the partisans. It was a generic term, an explanation in itself, like 'Chernobyl' or the 'Mafia'. From the day Helena fled with her family, the day of the Russian invasion in 1939, bands of villagers began to take to the forest. The forests here were wilderness, as impenetrable and wild as mountains. Only years after the end of the war did the last partisans finally re-emerge from them.

'Partisans,' repeated Pani Wala, 'the Red partisans burned it when the ground was hard, burned it and it was smoking for days . . .'

When the Germans invaded in 1941, the numbers of partisans increased. There were Polish partisans, Belorussian partisans, Jewish partisans, partisans with Bolshevik leanings, nationalist partisans. They fought as much amongst themselves as against Germans or Russians. During the German occupation, amongst the most effective were the Red partisans, backed by Russians. That put a date on it: after the Blitzkrieg of summer 1941. So the house was burnt that winter of 1941/42. Burn the nests, Lenin had said, and the birds will not come back.

Pani Wala stared ahead. The tears ran down her cheeks. The decades piled up behind her lips; she was unable to hold them back and all at once she was talking, in a trance-like monologue that was two parts poetry and one part song:

'*Boże, mój Boże*, what life there was then, picking raspberries and redcurrants and the pears you brought pears in your hat . . . on the tennis court the girls were singing and you with your books in the shade, you with your books and me darker than a beer-bottle and the dresses I made from Wilno cloth . . . But oh my God what happened what happened when the Russians came. . . you took the horses and fled, and the Germans came with their machines and the Russians were in the river . . . then the Russians came again and the Germans were in the river with their machines, drowning drowning like beasts in the river spread like leaves in the river . . .'

She paused. Zofia and I were silent.

'. . . Then the partisans at the window and the houses burning and who were they all who went into Russia . . . my Kazik bootless in the snow . . . God, my God and just last week the girl dead in the forest her breasts cut . . .'

Pani Wala turned and looked up at Zofia. Her eyes were red with tears. She took Zofia's hand in both of hers and gripped it fiercely. 'Pani Zofia, I will weep all night remembering you! You, Pani Zośka, with your little plaits and your bright face and the red dress I made with flamenco pleats . . .'

Pani Wala told us about an old woman living alone in the forest. Pani Jadzia, as she was known, had a wooden hut on the edge of a field of rye. Behind the hut was the forest. It was all very remote.

She was standing by her well when we arrived. Zofia explained who she was and Pani Jadzia nodded without smiling. She unhooked the bucket and started to carry it to the hut.

Yes, she remembered the Brońskis. She remembered her

sheep straying onto their land and Pan Adam finding them; she remembered him riding over, and her expecting his anger but instead he had asked about that year's lambs and sat and drank *kwas* with her father.

Pani Jadzia took her water inside and came out again into the sun. We sat on a bench against the wall and she looked at us both in turn.

She must have been well over eighty. Her head rose not upwards but forwards from the small mound of her shoulders. Her face was unmoving, set firm against the world. When she relaxed, as she did after her scrutinizing, you could tell she was smiling not because she smiled, but because there was a faint softening in her stony expression.

She told her story without sentiment. Many had told us how good the old life was, the life before the war. Pani Jadzia had no such illusions: it was all just as bad.

During the German occupation, she had been in the church one morning, the Gawja church a mile or so away. Walking home, she heard shooting. When she reached her home, the soldiers had already left. Her father, her mother, three brothers and two sisters were lying dead beside the beech trees.

Pani Jadzia paused, but her face remained expressionless.

Shortly after her family was killed, Pani Jadzia married. Her husband came to live with her in the forest. He helped her to take over the running of the sheep and the crops and the bees. Each week he rode into Nowogródek for supplies. One day he didn't come back; he'd been run over by a German tank. Then the Red partisans came out of the forest and burned everything.

Pani Jadzia married her second husband soon after the war. One evening someone leaned in through the window and shot him; there were rumours of some mistress or other. Her third husband was a drunk and she left him. Several years ago a herd of bison broke down her fence and trampled her plants and toppled her hives. Now she had only her bees and her dogs and a cow, and at hay-time her son came to help her. Yes, she said, God had blessed her with a fine son, a fine, strong and sturdy son who helped her at hay-time.

As we left she gave us a small jar of honey; I have never tasted such honey as Pani Jadzia's.

Back towards Mantuski, the pine forest closed in again. There was a group of villagers retrieving potatoes from an underground store.

'The dogs' grave,' whispered Zofia.

'What?'

'If they ask what we are doing, we say to them: "We are looking for the dogs' grave." There will be a hundred eyes watching us, ready to attack us!'

By this time, the silver had become almost an irrelevance to me. But it seemed churlish not to make some sort of effort.

'Now,' explained Zofia, 'on that morning, we heard the Russians had invaded at about five. Everyone was in a panic, running around like madmen. Mama and I went into the forest. We had the silver in mushroom baskets. We walked for about fifteen minutes and found a young plantation.'

We reached the ruins of the house again and stepped into the forest.

'Yes, it was in this direction. There were trees and then an open place, and then the plantation.'

The trees gave out sooner than Zofia was expecting. 'Ah . . . they must have cleared some of the forest here . . . That way! To the left.'

We skirted the edge of the field until we reached the trees on the far side. They were tall pine, laid out in ranks.

'This must be it!' said Zofia. 'The plantation! Now, seventeen for my age, forty-one for Mama's. The seventeenth row and the forty-first tree!'

I started to count. At seventeen, I cut across into the trees and was surrounded at once by that peculiar expectancy of the forest. The ridges were covered in a thick cushion of pine needles. Cobwebs hung in the still air. One or two trees had fallen, and their slender trunks lay slumped in the undergrowth. Where there were gaps the sun fell through the canopy, onto the forest floor like light into a cathedral.

Twenty-nine, thirty . . . At thirty-one, I reached a narrow track. Was it here fifty years ago?

I heard Zofia shouting from the edge of the plantation. 'There are people coming. Hurry!'

Beyond the track, the trees continued. Thirty-five, thirty-six – a gap at thirty-seven, thirty-nine, forty, forty-one.

'Hurry, Pheelip!'

A thick branch lay across the trench and this I broke. I dug down about two feet. The soil was soft and crumbly. There was nothing. I dug some more. Still nothing.

'Pheelip!'

Each stage of our walk here had diminished my faith in Zofia's navigation. That this was the right direction from the house, that it was the right plantation, that the rows had been left intact, that I had estimated the right number of trees, that fifty-three years had passed with the hoard not being found; all these things I doubted so much that, had it been there – had the silver candlesticks and salt cellars appeared gleaming among those roots – I honestly think the sheer improbability would have driven me mad.

I walked empty-handed back to Zofia. A group of three peasant men stood around her. She looked nervous.

'Nothing,' I said.

She turned to the men. 'The dogs' grave, you see. The . . . dogs' . . . grave.' But they weren't Polish and didn't understand. They leaned on their scythes. They scratched their heads.

One of them said something and the others laughed. We walked back through the trees.

It was a hot morning; flies hovered in the shafts of sunlight. Everything was brown and dusty. A cuckoo sounded from deep among the trees. We followed a sandy path that meandered through the pines, through the semi-darkness, and came out onto the banks of the river. The water stretched before us, brilliant and steely blue.

We walked a little way upstream. The forest fell away; the banks widened to a spongy sward. Zofia said, 'Oh isn't it beautiful, just as I remember it . . .'

Helena's papers were full of descriptions of this place; her love for it at times seemed almost to exceed that for her family. She used the forest like a palliative, the river like an oracle. She revived her spirits with the powerful tonic of the landscape. She escaped to it. Here, seeing it in the flesh, I could understand why.

On the opposite bank they were taking in the hay. A man was standing on the top of a cart spreading the grass. Others swayed through the fields with their scythes.

'Somewhere here,' said Zofia, 'we had a place . . . we always came to it at this time. Yes, there, in the trees!' A small burst of birch trees stood on the river's edge. Beyond it the river took a sharp turn to the left. 'We called it the Philosophers' Corner. We used to come here and talk – great big talks!'

'About what?'

'Oh, you know – life!' She pronounced it voluptuously – 'lye-ffe' – as though it were a favourite dish.

We sat on the bank by the trees. The sand martins twittered from across the water; others flew back and forth, dipping and diving over the river's languid stream.

'So,' she said, 'no house and no silver!' She did not sound disappointed.

'But these people that remember you?'

'Oh yes, that is worth much more.'

'Zosia,' I asked, 'do you know now why you had to come?'

She watched the river for a moment, then nodded.

'Why?'

'Curiosity.'

'That's all?'

'Yes.'

'Just curiosity?'

She paused. 'You know, if we'd found the silver and been killed by those peasants for it, it would have been because of my curiosity – I'm sorry! Women are more curious than men.'

'Really?'

'Listen, we used to play a game here.' She cupped her hands and shouted across the river: 'Kto zjadł jabłko z drzewa?' The echo came back from the far bank: 'eva, eva . . .' 'You see?'

'No.'

She smiled teasingly and shouted, louder this time: 'KTO ZJADL JABLKO Z DRZEWA . . . EVA . . . eva . . . va . . .'

'No!'

'"Who has eaten the apple of the tree?" And the echo comes "Eve"! You see, curiosity. She ate the apple out of curiosity.'

'And then look what happened!'

'Yes. Banished from the Garden. Just as we were.'

I asked if she really saw it as a vanished Eden.

'In a way, I do.'

'But it's a savage place.'

'Yes,' she said, 'that as well. A savage, damaged paradise.'

6

LATER THAT WEEK, Zofia and I went down to Lida to try and find the house of her grandparents. We found a *sovkhoz*, a vast collective farm. A sign marked the entrance with a name that had echoed through Zofia's childhood: KLEPAWICZE. The sign was a fine piece of Soviet kitsch, painted in a silvery, zinc-like paint and decorated, in bas relief, with a blooming flower, a wheat sheaf, a milk churn, a fat cow and a sickle.

Concrete buildings marked the core of the *sovkhoz* and on top of the largest was a digital read-out. The read-out changed every half minute or so – the time changed to the temperature, and the temperature changed to an enigmatic '10'.

'What's 10?' we asked.

'Not too bad . . .'

'No, what's it measuring?'

'Radiation –- Chernobyl.'

'Ugh!' said Zofia.

Off to one side of the new buildings was a small island of grass and lilac. In the middle of the island was a concrete bust of Lenin. He was in profile, thrusting out his chin towards the long classical front of a *dwór*.

'Yes, that's it,' said Zofia. 'That's the house!'

We stepped inside. To the right was the old drawing room. The walls were hung with purple drapes; there was a stage and a bank of electronics and two large speakers. On the purple drapes was fixed a series of plaster-cast images of more wheat sheaves, more fat cows, more milk churns.

The room, we were told, was the *sovkhoz* Marriage Palace. In other rooms were a dance floor, a clinic, and offices. Kind-faced women sat at empty desks, eager to make us tea, to talk, and to complain.

Upstairs was another series of offices. These had already been abandoned. Cabinets lay open, spilling years of files and quotas over the floor. In one of them, they lay so thickly you could not even see the boards. Dozens of posters, extolling the wonder of potatoes, the sin of drinking, lay among them. A pigeon had got into the room and flew hopelessly backwards and forwards: towards the light of the window, back into the darkness, towards the light, back into the dark. Several days of its droppings lay scattered over the *sovkhoz* files.

When we left the *sovkhoz*, the radiation clock read '12'.

Helena arrived at Klepawicze, for the first time, in the summer of 1914. She was sixteen. In the horse-drawn carriage, the leather seats were hot from the sun. The springs creaked beneath them. Every now and then a newspaper rustled opposite her, the newspaper of Pan Stanisław Broński, owner of Klepawicze. Grunts and pipe smoke rose above the paper; one shiny boot swung irritably back and forth beneath it.

Helena was furious. Her mother had announced to her only that morning that she was to spend two weeks with the Brońskis, a family she considered barbaric, medieval. But she knew she had no choice; such things were decided for her.

They drove on through the march of the Broński estate. When the forests thinned and the fields began, Pan Broński put down his paper and addressed Helena.

'Now, girl, what do you know of country things?'

'A little,' she said.

He stabbed a finger out of the window. 'So, what's that bird?' he asked.

Helena saw a large grey-white bird flying low, with a wave-like flight. 'A hen harrier?'

He nodded. 'A female. And the crop?'

Nothing was yet higher than a few inches, and all looked like young green grass.

'Rye.'

'Not barley?'

'No. It would not be up yet.'

Pan Broński raised an eyebrow and nodded. 'So she's no fool!'

The carriage pulled out of a long avenue of chestnuts and the road touched, like a tangent, the outer bend of the river. It was in spate: Helena could see the quick flow wrinkle as it buffed the near bank. One or two willows leaned over the water like shaggy anglers; beyond them were meadows, and the red-and-white cows knee-deep in sedge. Far downstream, the river made a deep 'V' in the forest.

'Oh, it's beautiful!' she cried and put a hand to her mouth. 'I'm sorry.'

Pan Broński glanced at her; he almost smiled.

The road headed towards a low wall and a pair of griffin-topped gate-posts. Running beneath them, the carriage crunched across the gravel. There was an oval of lawn in front of the house.

The horses came to a halt. The four Broński brothers, dressed alternately in dark coats and army uniforms, had lined up to meet them. Two sisters stood on the terrace behind them. Pan Broński stepped down from the carriage and his sons took it in turns to kiss his hand.

'Had I known then', Helena wrote, years later, 'that one of those boys, fawning on their father, would end up as my husband, I think I would have gone to find the nearest convent.'

At dinner that evening Helena sat next to Pan Broński. His boyar-like presence dominated the room. The meal was almost over when he turned to Helena for the first time, smiled, and asked her about her interests.

'Reading,' she said. 'I enjoy history.'

'Reading's no good for a woman. You want to know the three qualities for a really good wife?' He held up three fingers and counted them off. 'Ugly, poor and stupid.'

The table fell silent.

He continued. 'Ugly, so no other man will look at her; poor, so she will need you for money; and stupid so she will not outwit you!'

Half-way down the room came a hiss of black silks, and Pan Broński's wife stood and ran in tears from the table.

Broński took up his glass. 'Dear me,' he said, 'whatever is the matter with her?'

The hours at Klepawicze marched past Helena with the precision of a military parade. Everything was strictly ordered. She spent what time she could out of doors: her love for the outdoors just about compensated for the darkness inside. On the third morning she left the house and entered the woods.

The ground was thick with summer growth. One or two mushrooms stood out like shot silk from the ivy below. Stepping through it, Helena listened to the wind flowing through the oak, to the chatter of finches, the caw of a crow and, from deep among the trees, the sound of a cuckoo. She was swept up in a surge of high spirits and, leaping into an exuberant dance, broke into song:

> *Karolina Niemka,*
> *To nasza panienka!*
> *Karolina rączkę daje*
> *Pojedziemy w cudze kraje.*

A voice came through the trees. 'What a pretty, fluffy little gosling!' And from behind a beech appeared Wincenty Broński. He was grinning. Without a word Helena ran back to the house.

The Broński brothers stalked the corners of Klepawicze like satyrs. Wincenty was the third son. He spent much of the day in his wicker chair, reading. He had caught pneumonia when studying in Kiev: his father had refused him money for a winter coat. The pneumonia had become TB, and he had recently lost a lung. Two years after her visit, wrote Helena, he had died.

Of the three other brothers, Adam was the eldest. He paid little attention to Helena. He would walk up and down the lime avenues lost in thought, or play the piano for hours on end. Being the eldest he had not been called to the army, but was required instead to oversee his land.

Theodore, on the other hand, lived for his Uhlan regiment. He had learned some spectacular tricks, and passed much of the day practising them, leaping up on a cantering horse, plucking stakes from the ground at a gallop, standing in the saddle while clapping his hands.

On one occasion he managed to catch Helena, scoop her up in front of his saddle-bow, and whisk her off to the smoke-house. There, among the brick-red hams and bacon flitches he subjected her to a smoky kiss. He then locked her in. Only a passing gardener who heard her cries after three hours ensured her release, but her white dress was ruined by the smoke.

Ignatius, the youngest, did not register Helena's presence at all. He was taciturn and moody. Exempt from military duty on account of a paralysed arm, he ran through the corridors, chasing his sisters with a horse-whip. His deformity, wrote Helena, was the result of his father forcing him to ride an unbroken stallion. Pan Broński had also killed Ignatius's pet rabbit when he was seven. Grown too fond of it, he explained, then forced the boy to eat it.

Such was the currency of affection at Klepawicze.

*   *   *

Helena spent most of the fortnight either on her own or with the two Broński sisters – Ziuta and Wanda. One day they rose early and set off on a long ride. It was a bright morning and the sand martins were flying high above the river.

Ziuta led them through the meadows and up on to the high banks beyond. One or two skiffs arced across the river, loaded with cattle feed and fencing posts, and one with a large red-and-white bull.

At the first bend, the three of them cut inland. They cantered past the sprouting rye fields, kicked up saucers of dried mud from the track, then took a green path which wound in amongst the trees.

All morning they rode deeper into the forest. They saw only a few woodmen and loggers, and after an hour no one at all. It was about midday when through the trees came the 'thud, thud' of an axe. They entered a clearing. Three wagons were arranged side-on around a large fire. Sooty-faced children ran up to the horses and beat their legs with sticks.

'Stop that!'

On the steps of the nearest wagon was an elderly woman in a brightly coloured apron; a large lump of amber swung from her neck as she stepped down.

Ziuta whispered, 'It is Marucha! She is a famous clairvoyant!'

Marucha peered up at them. 'What have you got for me?'

The Brońskas each produced a silver rouble. Helena fumbled in her pocket and came out with the gold five-rouble piece her mother had given her for the return journey. Marucha took it and turned it over. Then she smiled and pointed to a bench beside the fire.

Helena was worried her gold coin would prejudice the gypsy's verdict, but in years to come, when she thought of that gypsy camp, and what was said, she discovered a strange truth in Marucha's predictions.

'You have a hand with all the graces and saving signs.'

Marucha traced her finger across Helena's palm. 'I see a pine alone on the steppe, strong and unafraid, but a lonely pine, always lonely. There is a small copse of saplings around it, and now there comes a great fire. There are men with axes, but I cannot see their faces. They do not reach the saplings, and the fire remains a little way off.'

Next she took Ziuta's hand and said it showed an identical life and identical upbringing. 'But here the pine is twisted and crowded by others. And now, the fire comes and also the men with axes, and the crooked pine is gone.'

Helena gripped Ziuta's arm and said, in English, 'Don't worry. It is just nonsense!'

But when the great fire did come, more than a quarter of a century later, Ziuta, the wife of a Polish general, was captured and died in a damp Soviet cell.

Marucha produced a pack of cards. She handed them to Helena who cut them and handed them back.

'Think of who is in your heart, girl, and then think of a card.'

Ziuta leaned forward. 'Who is it? Please, Hela, whisper!'

Helena mentioned Józef, their cousin, an intense, dark-haired man who had danced twice with her and taken her skating once in Wilno. To her, this was unquestionably love.

Marucha scanned the cards. When she stretched out her hand it fell on the Jack of Clubs.

'You chose him?'

Helena nodded. 'How did you know?'

'*On ciebie do ołtarza poprowadzi*. This man', she waved the card, 'will lead you to the altar.'

On the day of Helena's wedding in 1920, Wilno was taken by the Red Army. Few were able to reach the church at Platków. It fell to Józef, the Broński's cousin, to lead Helena up the aisle, and give her away to her husband.

*   *   *

From Klepawicze, Zofia and I drove on into the forest. After several kilometres we reached a cemetery. On an obelisk, in the middle of the cemetery, were chiselled the names of Brońskis – Władysławs and Józefs, Marias and Irenas.

'Aunts and uncles,' said Zofia vaguely.

'But here, Zosia, Stanisław Broński. Isn't that your grandfather?'

'Yes . . .' Yet she was looking not at the obelisk, but at the steps below it which led down towards the vault.

'Pheelip, dear, will you go down? I don't think I could manage with my plastic hips.'

I started down the steps. At the bottom was a broken wooden door, some fallen masonry and beyond it, darkness.

'What can you see?' Zofia shouted.

'Nothing. It's pitch dark!'

I pushed past the door and waited a moment while my eyes became used to the dark. Underfoot, the ground was covered in rubble; the blocks moved as I stepped over them and into the mouth of the vault.

'Anything at all?' cried Zofia.

'Nothing.'

'What did you say?'

'Nothing, Zosia! I can't see anything!'

'Oh!'

I knew she was still curious. I tore some pages from my notebook and, twisting them into faggots, went further into the vault. The tomb had been looted; that had been clear when we first saw it. Zofia had shrugged it off. What can you expect? That the old world had been shattered the moment she left, she accepted now as something inevitable.

I lit the paper. The flame sent a yellow light into the darkness. It flickered on the low ceiling and cast deep shadows beyond the broken masonry on the floor. Slatted shelves ran along one wall. But they were broken too, and in the corner their half-burned timbers fanned out from the ashes of an old fire.

'Pheelip!' Zofia's cries were more distant now. 'Can you see?'

'Yes!'

'What is there?'

'Wait . . .'

'Any bones?'

My feet slid between the blocks. To one side, amidst the masonry, was a pile of copper coffins.

'Coffins, Zosia!'

Stepping over the debris, I could see the detailing, the swags on the patinaed lids, the panelling on the sides. I could also see the large holes that had been blasted in the copper shells.

Zofia's voice came echoing down into the vault: 'Are they open or closed?'

'Open.'

'Have a look inside, will you?'

Inside? I took another rolled-up paper, lit it from the first and held it over one of the holes. In order to see in I had to press my chin down almost to the metal, and holding the flame as close as possible, peer sideways at the interior. After several seconds, the shapes inside began to take on form. There were bones: ribs and vertebrae and the tatters of ancient cloth. I looked into the others; the same thing.

Back at the surface, Zofia said, 'What do you think, Pheelip? We could take some of the bones with us. Maybe we could bury them again in Cornwall?'

I pictured going back in and extracting them; I pictured Soviet customs; I pictured a plot in some benign creek-side Cornish graveyard, thousands of miles from here, a world away from these trampled borderlands. I suggested we leave them.

Zofia looked up into the trees. She was smiling. 'You know, I think I can hear them all laughing – all the ghosts of my ancestors looking down at us, and laughing!'

7

THOSE WEEKS in Belorussia passed quickly. They were brightly coloured, packed with a strange intensity. Each encounter, each story seemed to contain in it a lifetime of incident. Often, looking out of the car window as we drove, Zofia would shake her head and say, 'I can't believe this. I can hardly believe I'm here.'

Before returning to Minsk we managed to spend one more afternoon at Mantuski. It was a hot day. We walked down to Philosophers' Corner and sat in the shade of the birch trees. The Niemen slid idly past our feet. We opened the bottle of expedition vodka and drank and talked of various things. Then I dozed off and woke to find that Zofia had written a sonnet. I asked her to translate it.

She cleared her throat. '"I sit by the Niemen and look" – no, "gaze – at the boats . . . offspring of crows cackle behind me . . . same woods, same meadows . . . decades have gone . . . and now this wordless enchantment – this loss, this sadness, this surprise –"'

She glanced up from the page. 'No . . . "zdumienie". It's stronger than surprise . . . "amazement".' She read on: '". . . what became of that water, what became of the time . . . spell-binding – self-absorbed – full flood tickling my stars and my fish. I hurry on to the sea, as this is my fate."'

She looked at the river. 'It's odd. Here I seem to be able to write only in this canon of loss. And only in Polish.'

Later in the evening, our friends the doctor and his family came over from Iwje for a picnic. We drove through the forest, coming out of the trees further upstream. *Kolkhoz* cattle were scattered in the meadows on the opposite bank. The doctor's wife unloaded food from the car; the rest of us went into the forest to collect wood.

The doctor was in high spirits. 'In your country, you cannot do this. You cannot come and take wood from the forest! Everything belongs to someone, am I not right? But here we have socialism! Socialism! After all, who can such a forest belong to?'

I winked at Zofia. 'You!'

It was dusk by the time the fire was hot enough to cook the potatoes. The smoke rose in the still air and tangled in the fringes of the forest. The doctor's wife unwrapped from newspaper a Niemen pike; the doctor bit the plastic stopper off a bottle of vodka and spat it out. The *kolkhoz* cows were driven up out of the meadows, onto drier pasture. The river pressed on to the west.

A little later, full of pike and potatoes, and full of vodka, Zofia and I left the others and walked along the river. The moon was red and bulbous above the forest. The soft croaking of a woodcock came from the trees; the only other sound was the distant chatter from around the fire.

Zofia stopped, looking up along the banks. 'Fifty years I have struggled to keep this place alive . . .'

The curls of her grey hair had been tousled by our travels; her eyes, sad and hooded as always, were calm. 'Now it all comes back.' She smiled. 'I remember in the winter the noises the ice on the river made – cracking like gunshots. And here, I used to come riding. There was one day in particular. I was about fourteen and had a pony called Delilah. I tied her up over there. There was no one about, so I took off all my clothes and went swimming. That was forbidden, of course! But my mother was away and I remember thinking then, here on the river, that suddenly anything was possible.'

She paused. 'How strange it is, that day seems to me now like the beginning of the world.'

We returned to Minsk. On our last evening, the last evening in Belorussia, we were invited to a 'Poets' Evening' at the Dom Literatury.

'What do you think that means, Pheelip, a "Poets' Evening?"'

'I've no idea, Zosia.'

We gathered in an upper room with about twenty or thirty others. After a series of readings, a song, more readings, more songs, there were the speeches. Everyone made a speech – speeches to poets, speeches by poets, speeches to wine-making, to poetry, to the new era of independence, to Belorussia. I was asked to make a speech and spoke about nationalism and its dangers, about the risks as I saw them of new fault-lines emerging in Europe – until I realized no one understood a word of English. Zofia had a little more luck with her Polish.

'I am a Pole,' she announced, 'who fled my country when the Russians invaded in 1939 and now I have come back to see what happened. My mother lived in Minsk for a while in 1918 and she fled too. She was in love in Minsk but the Bolsheviks came and drove her away. And now they have gone, I can come back. Perhaps we should drink to that!' She picked up her glass and everyone followed suit, nodding in agreement.

'But I would also like to say something else.' Zofia placed her glass back on the table. 'I too am a poet. I have written verse now for more than fifty years. Yet in my writing I am a traitor. I have betrayed the greatest thing a poet is given – her own language. I had to abandon my beloved Polish and now I write poems in English and I feel like a bigamist . . . The only Belorussian I know is a rhyme I learnt as a child.' (She recited the comic circular rhyme which she had told me, years earlier, concerning a priest and his dead dog. No one knew it. There was much applause.) 'So I would like to drink a toast to the end of communism, to a new era, to poetry, to friendship, and to the Slavic soul which we all share and which seems to me to gravitate so beautifully between vodka and tears. *Na zdrowie!*'

Na zdrowie!

Everyone clapped and drank. There were more speeches. A woman made a speech about Mickiewicz. A professor made a speech about politics. (They were all wearing tiny red-and-white badges on their lapels, the colours of their brand-new country for which they – the poets, the writers, the intellectuals – were trying to mould something distinctive from the heavy brown clay of Soviet culture.)

The professor was still speaking when the meal began. Spontaneously the poets leaned forward and colonized the plates of food. The professor gave up on his point about public spending and grabbed a sausage, two pieces of bread and a gherkin.

Zofia had recovered her good spirits; she was giggling. Opposite her a man in a black shirt, with a gold-toothed flashing smile, slopped vodka into her glass. 'Drink! Drink, my jewelled Polish princess!'

She turned to me and whispered, 'He thinks I am a princess. He has translated Verlaine and says he is in love with me! What do I do?'

'I think you'd better marry him, Zosia.'

At the other end of the table a Romanian folk singer raised herself from her chair. She shrieked a song in Belorussian. When it was over, a tiny old woman stood up beside her. This old woman, with egg-yolk hair and an emerald-green cardigan, had apparently been a famous opera singer. She trotted out an unknown aria in a cracked soprano, and then said, 'I am ninety-two. All my life has been dedicated to beauty.'

Another couple stood, fair-skinned and fair-haired. She was wearing a headscarf, he a buttoned-up mud-brown suit.

'For twenty year,' she explained, 'he is in prison. I think

him dead, in camp. Then he came to my door the week ago,
and knock and say, Marta, I need some water. I am thirsty.
Where have you been? I ask. And he is weeping like a
child . . .'

Beside her, this man, spruce-straight and a foot taller than
her, flicked the tears from his cheek as if they were pebbles.

A woman with an accordion started the dancing; people stood
and soon the whole room was a mass of reeling, bobbing poets.
The wild-faced lexicographer and the nervous teacher, the expert
on Bernard Shaw, the toothless archaeologist dancing alone, a
famous actress, a leaping linguist, a balding translator of Dante,
an earnest young guitarist with sad songs, and Zofia with her
Belorussian 'husband', her 'Don Juan'.

The evening subsided into a haze of vodka and *żubrówka* and
tearful speeches and stories. It was after midnight when people
began to slip away. The lexicographer was asleep in a chair.
The archaeologist was standing on one leg. The nonagenarian
opera singer was carried out by her daughter the accordion
player. The actress was weeping. Zofia was having her palm
read by Don Juan.

'Don't throw your love to the dogs!' he pleaded – adding,
in a whisper, 'My wife, she has the tongue of a viper . . .' Then
he cried, 'Our meeting it was written in the stars! Such joy I
have not known like this evening . . .'

'But you,' said Zofia, tapping his chest with her finger, 'you
are a Slav like me – and tomorrow you'll be sad.'

Three days later, we crossed the border and arrived back in
Warsaw. It was five in the morning and we were both exhausted.
At the railway station we bickered, pointlessly – about where
to get a taxi, about whether Warsaw was dirty or not, about
the exact date of the Yalta conference – until Zofia threw back
her head and laughed, 'Look how foolish we are, Pheelip. We're
just tired!' And soon we were in a taxi, winding through empty

streets to the Dom Literatury: another town, another Dom Literatury.

We took rooms there and stayed several days, resting, reading, writing notes, seeing friends and having earnest debates with various writers. Our rooms looked over the cobbled square in front of the palace, over the Vistula, over the roofs of the suburbs to the forest beyond. The city that May seemed full of light.

On the plane home, Zofia said she felt she had 'closed the circle'. That was why she had come all this way – to close the circle.

London was thundery and humid. We left the airport and took a bus into town. Our journey was over. At Paddington we stood together on the platform while heavy rain drummed the station roof. Zofia was going home to Cornwall; I was staying in London.

'I will miss you,' she said. 'These last weeks have been incredible to me.'

'For me too.'

She reached up and traced a cross on my forehead. 'I leave you with an angel. May everything go well for you, dear Pheelip!'

It was November before I moved back to Cornwall for the winter. In the evenings, I went up to Braganza and sat with Zofia and we drank home-made *żubrówka*, distilled by a Polish cook in one of the local villages. Zofia remained poised in her high-backed chair, her face its usual medley of expressions, while we talked about pre-war Poland, about her mother's reminiscences, about our own journey. At Christmas, we put together parcels of chocolates and clothes for Pani Wala and Pani Jadzia and the watchmaker – which never reached them.

In the meantime, Braganza's bookshelves proved a jig-saw of Polish history: memoirs, poetry and novels, each volume adding a piece to the context of Zofia's first life. Poland appeared in all its various guises – Poland as history's plaything, Poland both conquering and conquered, Poland as the perennial survivor; Poland where personal lives seemed no more than a light diversion between wars, like a game played while waiting for a train.

'*Polot,*' said Zofia. 'It all comes down to *polot.*'

'*Polot?*'

'It doesn't translate. "Lot" means flight, of course, like the Polish airline, and there is a sense of weightlessness about it. But it's also a certain charm, a panache – something to do with being dashing and brave – appearing to fly through hardship!'

'And your mother had *polot?*'

'Oh yes. She had *polot.*'

In her *Lost in Translation*, Eva Hoffman cites two instances of *polot*. The first was in 1939, when the German Panzer divisions rolled into Poland, and the Poles, refusing to surrender, rode at the tanks with their cavalry. Then during the Warsaw rising of 1944, while the Nazis were flushing out the last pockets of resistance, the Poles erected speakers in the streets and played Chopin.

Other incidents from Polish history stayed with me. There was the victory message that King Jan Sobieski sent to the Pope after the Siege of Vienna: 'Venimus, Vidimus, Deus Vicit.' And the observation of an Allied observer sent to Warsaw in 1945: the place he said was full of flower stalls – not a building intact, rubble everywhere, bread beyond the means of most, but flowers, stalls and stalls of fresh flowers from the fields.

And the old Polish joke (the favourite, it is said, of Paderewski, Prime Minister of newly liberated Poland in 1919): a professor at an international college sets his students a long dissertation on the general theme of 'The Elephant'. The titles come back as follows:

The Englishman: The Elephant, and how to hunt him.
The Frenchman: The Love-life of the Elephant.

> The German (after much research): An Introduction to
> the Preliminary Study of the Gastronomic Possibili-
> ties of the Elephant.
> The Russian (after anguished smoking of cigarettes):
> The Elephant – does he exist?
> The Pole: The Elephant and the Polish Question.

But the story that remained sharpest concerned the unveiling
of a statue of Adam Mickiewicz in Warsaw. Like Pushkin,
Mickiewicz is a national poet and his statue was to be a national
monument. The time of the unveiling was shortly after the
Polish Uprising of 1863, and the Russian governor was nervous.
He wheeled up his artillery, knocking down several rows of
buildings as he did so. Tens of thousands of Poles had gathered
in the square. Henryk Sienkiewicz stepped up to the podium.
From his pocket he took the pages of a speech he had been
forbidden to make. He waved the pages in the wind. There
was silence. He unveiled the statue. Still silence. The Russians
stared at the Poles and the Poles stared at the Russians. Not a
sound.

Then from the midst of the crowd was heard the noise of a
woman sobbing. Then another, and another until all that could
be heard in the centre of Warsaw, on the occasion of the
unveiling of Mickiewicz's statue, was a low collective wailing.

Mickiewicz was born in Nowogródek. Just off the town's
main square is the Dom Mickiewicza, a museum to his memory.
Zofia said her mother used to go there in 1915 each Sunday
after Mass, and found in her papers this description:

> The Mickiewicz house was lived in and run by two women.
> On Sunday they gave great feasts for anyone who wanted
> to come. The women never had a rouble between them
> but every time they wanted money they just went to Uncle
> Nicholas. One of the women had a squint and was known

for her good works and frequent bouts of praying. The other had little brown curls and lay on the sofa eating chocolates and reading romances. She eventually swelled to twenty stone and tyrannized her companion . . .

One morning in Nowogródek, Zofia and I had tried to visit the Dom Mickiewicza. It had recently been restored but that morning it was closed, surrounded by fallen trees. A storm in the night had left the whole town choked with fallen trees. (Fallen trees: Helena had been born on the night of the great storm in 1898, and it had taken years to clear the trees.)

From Braganza, I retrieved Helena's papers, the notebooks, the loose typed sheets, the newspaper cuttings. They came to me in a box marked 'GEEST BANANAS'. One morning in January – a morning of high winds prodding at the eaves of my cottage, of restless waves tearing at the beach below – I dipped into the box and took out the first of these notebooks. The corners were scuffed slightly, and one had been chewed by something, a mouse or a dog. The book was a burgundy red and on its front cover Zofia had stuck a label: 'recycled paper – THIS LABEL SAVES TREES'. Beneath it she had written: 'Mama's Life vol I'.

Inside, the title was echoed in her mother's own hand:

My Own Life – volume I

When I look back at my life it is chiefly a strange loneliness that is its mark. I was a lonely child – without friends or companions – a child who somehow had no personal life, was hardly aware of existing so engrossed was she in the lives of her animals and her friends who were all grown-ups – aunts, Panna Konstancja, all the people of Platków, and Mother Immaculate.

I grew up very late, was happy and adored in St Petersburg, chased from one place to the next by war, lonely in marriage, and finally happy alone at Mantuski . . .

Re-reading Helena's papers that winter, two things, two patterns, seemed to emerge. One was the strange symmetry between her own circumstances and the wider turbulence around her (the parade of her suitors, for instance, during the years after the first war appeared to mirror the comings and goings of armies). The other was a sense of constant change, the work of unseen forces: precisely the feeling that comes from seeing trees scattered by the wind.

For sixteen years, Helena led a life of relative calm. But one lunch-time in the summer of 1914, at Klepawicze, all that came to an end.

PART II

HELENA

8

EACH DAY AT KLEPAWICZE, in that summer of 1914, a table was set on the verandah for lunch. Jugs of lemonade and *kwas* stood next to a ham or a side of cold beef. There were plates of cheese and chives and always a vase of peonies. Helena and the Broński sisters gathered there first, then the brothers and at precisely 12.45 p.m., Pan Stanisław would appear from his study, say Grace and the meal would begin.

One day during the second week of Helena's stay Pan Stanisław was late. It was after one o'clock before he stepped out through the French windows, poured himself a glass of *kwas* and announced that the Kaiser had declared war.

There was silence. Helena looked at the Broński sisters and at the brothers, at the various aunts and retainers. What did war mean? Their faces gave no clue.

After lunch she walked down to the river. She sat beneath a stand of birches. Swallows gave out a continuous squeaking from across the water. She lay back on the grass and closed her eyes. The sun glowed bright orange behind her eyelids. If she moved her head, the birch branches broke the sunlight and the world was full of orange flashing. She heard the guns and saw the charging horses. She saw columns of men and rows of uniforms. That was war.

The following day she was sent back home to Wilno. Everything there was just the same as before – a few more horses perhaps, a few more troops, a few more people in church – but that was all. Then after a few weeks came the defeat at Tannenburg and people said that the war might not be over quite so soon.

* * *

One evening in October, Count O'Breifne appeared at the house in Wilno for a few days' leave. He called Helena to his library at 9.30 the next morning. Turned away from his desk, he was looking out of the window. A bright autumn light was falling into the room, brushing the side of his face. His feet were apart and he was toying with his fingers behind his back.

'Father?'

He turned to face her. He looked tired. His skin was loose and his lips pale; he had the appearance of someone waiting for an operation. But he smiled, and stepped in out of the light.

Instead of kissing her, he said, 'Helenka, look at you! You're a mess!'

Tugging down her shirt, he shook his head. He made her straighten her skirt. Then he sat down wearily behind his desk. 'I must talk to you, Helena. You are no longer a girl. You are fifteen—'

'Sixteen, Father.'

'Sixteen?'

'Yes.'

'Well, it's time you learnt.' He raised his eyebrows and sighed. 'Hela, you must understand that a woman has to dress well. It is her duty to look her best.'

It was the first time he had ever addressed her as anything other than a child.

'You see,' he continued, 'the happiness and well-being of a family depends on the woman. If she makes an effort constantly, her husband will remain attached to her. A man in love with his wife will always make a good father. You have been brought up to believe it is a virtue not to think of your looks, not to care about clothes. Is that not right?'

She nodded.

'My dear Hela, it is not a virtue – but a crime. Your poor mother was brought up by a man, a saintly man, who knew nothing of women. Her utter lack of feminine charm has brought misery to us both. She should not have married at all. She has no use for marriage. Marriage is based on physical ties and your mother cares nothing for that.'

He was holding a paper-knife and he flicked some imaginary dust from his ink-pad. Helena remained silent.

'You must not fall into the same trap. I don't know how long I will be here to help you, but you must promise me to try? Will you do that?'

'Yes, Father.'

He stood and came round the desk. He took each of her hands. 'You are beautiful, my Helenka. You are a Diane Chasseusse, a Juno . . .'

Helena tried to look away.

'But please don't waste it! Don't wear these horrible little buttons and frills. You must dress in straight and simple lines. Don't you think you'd feel happier in such clothes?'

'I have nothing of that kind.'

'I know, I know. It is wartime, and your mother says it is not the time to buy good clothes. Is that not right?'

Helena smiled. 'Yes, Tatuś!'

He turned and went across the room and entered a door in the bookshelves. When he came back he held a pile of boxes. He placed them on the desk in front of Helena.

'I bought these for you in St Petersburg. Go on,' he said, 'open them.'

She untied the uppermost box, and peeled back the folds of tissue. There was a tailored riding habit inside. In the next box was a hat wrapped in heavy white silk and fixed with a tiny bunch of violets. In the next was a long wine-red coat. In another was a whole set of thin summer frocks, and a yellow-striped pinafore, and an evening gown of pale pink silk. There were boxes of shoes and belts and gloves.

Helena looked up at her father.

'Try them on.'

She went through the bookshelf door, into his dressing room. She set down the boxes. The room had her father's smell. In the middle of it was a tall looking-glass, which pivoted in the middle and Helena pushed it down to see herself. He was right – she looked a mess!

She tried on all the clothes, then re-entered the library in the evening gown.

'Now, enough of these ponytails!' Her father slipped off her hair clasp. He gathered her hair and reassembled it on top of her head. One or two fronds twisted down her temple.

'Look, you see?' he said.

'Thank you, Tatuś.'

'Don't worry.' He bent to kiss her forehead. 'I will explain it all to your mother.'

Her mother thought him mad. She said it was a sin to spend so much on clothes. Now, at this time! Ach! But seeing that his furlough in Wilno was so brief, she let the matter drop.

It was the middle of May, 1915. In Wilno the trees had burst into flower; white lilac and bird-cherry crowded the streets with their bridal blooms; the parks were spotted with camomile. Helena grew restless. She wrote of a sense of undirected excitement, a physical feeling. Something was approaching and she could not see it, she could not touch it, she did not know its name. It had nothing to do with the war. Did everyone feel like this? She had no idea. She had no one to ask.

At times the feeling of expectancy was overwhelming. On slow afternoons she took to walking alone through the town, blinking in the strange light, constantly alert, constantly surprised by familiar things. For her, spring never came again without bringing back something of May 1915.

On most days there was a wind. In the avenues it swept through the rowan trees with a sound like water; it tugged at the horse-chestnuts; it set the fat fingers of their leaves flopping to and fro. Helena took in the sweet-and-sour smells of Wilno's markets, the shouts of the hawkers, the slinking forms of tinkers. At midday she felt fiercely alive; by late afternoon she was exhausted.

In the evening a cooler wind brought the sound of church bells. She toured the chapels, praying, indulging her earnest and precocious piety, gazing at the Miraculous Madonna of the Ostra Brama. The sacrament was exposed in all of Wilno's churches. People spilled out of the pews, standing shoulder-to-shoulder, cramming the west doors. Men squeezed their caps in knotted fists; women knelt in the aisles. All sent their eager prayers drifting upwards – urging God to hold back the Germans.

The Russians were in retreat. From the west came reports of whole villages fleeing. All over the country, households were sending their livestock east, away from the hands of the Kaiser. Journeymen told of roads choked with guns and muddy soldiers and herds of lolloping beasts.

One afternoon Helena was standing on the balcony. A hay cart turned off the main road and into Mała Pohulanka. Behind the cart was another cart, then a larger wagon and a string of brood-mares attached to it; their clumsy-footed foals trotted beside them. Helena recognized her grandmother's troupe of Lithuanian Zmudziaki horses; it was then she knew that they would all have to leave.

The O'Breifnes went south at first. The horses were sent on ahead. Their own party, six of them, travelled by train: Helena's mother, Helena, her brother and sister – both much younger – Panna Konstancja and Tekla.

Over the coming years, Panna Konstancja and Tekla accompanied the family wherever they went. Panna Konstancja was a large, matronly figure with a sharp tongue and a roguish humour. She, almost alone, had brought up Helena; she was a much less distant figure than her own mother. Tekla was the family's cook, the fatherless child of a 'corner-woman' taken in by Helena's mother.

A thirty-five-kilometre drive took the party from the station at Nowojelnia to Druków. It was a drowsy evening. The heads of the horses were heavy, bullied by flies. Helena's mother fanned herself with a book. Tekla had acute diarrhoea and there were frequent stops.

Helena felt daunted by this retreat. Would it end at Druków? What if the Germans like Napoleon could not be stopped and they were pushed on, deeper into Russia? The east! Russia! Helena baulked suddenly at the thought of the snowy steppe, the grey hills, the unkempt beards of the Orthodox priests, the rows of high-cheeked Tartars against the snow. Then she fell asleep in the familiar regions of Panna Konstancja's chest.

When she woke they were almost there. The driver clicked his tongue and the horses turned off the road and into Druków's twisting avenue. Tekla made a final leap from the *bryczka* and ran for a bush.

Druków was the home of Uncle Nicholas O'Breifne, a softly spoken, bookish man who had never had children and treated Helena as his own. They spent much of that summer at Druków.

It was a quiet summer; news of the war punctuated it only rarely. Helena spent much of her time – when not in her mother's makeshift classes – walking or riding. She walked with Uncle Nicholas out beyond the avenue. She loved to hear him name the trees and flowers, identify the call of each bird.

One afternoon they returned via the Druków church. Inside it was cool and dark. In silence, the two of them stepped up to the chancel and knelt – Uncle Nicholas huge and barrel-shaped in his old camlet coat, Helena slim beside him with a blue velvet ribbon in the tangle of her hair.

Uncle Nicholas pointed out the commemorative plaques to his father, his grandfather and other O'Breifnes.

'Uncle Nicholas,' she asked, 'have your family lived here for a very long time?'

The first O'Breifne at Druków, he explained, was the General; he would have been her great-grandfather. The Russians were very proud of him, even though he was not Russian. In Serbia he had once saved the Russian army from the Turks. On the night before the battle a nun named Dovergill had come and warned him that the Turks would attack the following day. He prepared his positions well and was victorious. But when the general asked in the neighbouring convents for Dovergill, he drew a blank. 'Dovergill? Devorgil? There is no nun by that name.'

Only later did he find out who she was – an ancestor of his, an Irish queen of the twelfth century. She had been abducted by the King of Leinster and the row that followed led to the invasion of the Normans. This, said Uncle Nicholas, was the beginning of the end for the ancient Irish kings and chiefs. Four centuries later, they suffered their final defeat at the Battle of the Boyne, when the O'Briefnes themselves fled Ireland to end up in Russia.

General O'Breifne, he continued, bought Druków and its five thousand souls. The serfs were mainly Polish Catholics. One day he rode down to inspect the estate. He found a great number of them in church. A Mass was being said. The general strode in just in time to hear an anxious petition raised to protect them all from the 'Russian general' who had bought them. General O'Breifne walked up the aisle. His spurs clanked on the stone floor. He knelt at the front. The priest fell silent.

'Carry on,' the general said, and the priest stammered on through the liturgy.

'When the Mass was over the general rose from his knees and turned to face the congregation. "Please, there is no need to fear. I am not Russian. My name is O'Breifne and I am a

Catholic. I come from a very old Catholic country – a country far to the west called Ireland." '

O'Breifne meant nothing to them, nor Ireland, and they were not at all convinced by this foreigner and his strange name.

'Only when he returned with a Polish wife', said Uncle Nicholas, 'did the people begin to believe him.'

Klepawicze was no more than a few hours' ride away from Druków and Adam Broński was a frequent visitor. He was closely involved with the Polish underground movement and, wrote Helena, had the unquestioning respect of the peasants.

Though he completely ignored her, one thing about Adam made a particular impression on Helena at that time: he seemed utterly oblivious to rank. Her mother found this very strange. He appeared to come to Druków more to be with the land agent than with the O'Breifnes.

'Wartime, dear. Farmers are very important in wartime. Adam must do his duty.' And because he had such good manners, was the heir to Klepawicze, and was the son of Pan Stanisław Broński, she forgave him.

One morning, Adam rode over to help the agent clean the carp pond. Helena sat on the bank and watched. The two men opened the sluices and Adam stripped to the waist. He bent to pick the wriggling fish from the mud.

'Breeding!' he cried, or, 'Cooking!' and threw the fish into one or other of two galvanized bowls.

After lunch Helena stood before the high mirror in her bedroom. How could she get Adam to talk to her? Panna Konstancja had said if she made herself smart for once, she might be surprised.

She picked up her hairbrush. She pulled it down through her long auburn hair. It would not fall straight; she wanted it straight! But with each stroke of the brush its stubborn curl sent it springing back. She threw the brush down.

In the wardrobe were the Petersburg clothes her father had given her. She pinned her hopes on a dress of sky-blue cotton and a straw hat. Chewing a cherry to colour her lips, she went out into the park.

Beyond the drive was a small birch copse. Helena said she heard Adam's voice echoing through the trees. She stood on the edge of the copse and pulled back the leaves to see in. He was alone. Now he would talk to her!

He was standing there beneath the trees, singing. He did not see her. He broke into a strange Indian dance. He threw open his arms and spun. He tried a one-legged pirouette but fell to the ground.

Helena could not help smiling. But she remained where she was. She watched him get up. She watched him run backwards and forwards through the trees. He did not once look in her direction. Soon he had run off into the distance. She waited for him to come back, but he did not. She returned to the house in silence. She threw her hat on the bed. What a waste of time it all was! Animals, as she always suspected, were much less bothersome.

9

IN THE DINING ROOM at Druków one wall was painted with a scene of Diana hunting in the Arician grove. Each morning, at breakfast, a samovar was placed against this scene. It filled the room with strange bubbling noises and Panna Konstancja would come in, wink at Helena, and cock an ear to the samovar: *'German idyot . . . German idyot . . .* Do you hear, Hela? The Germans are coming!'

And the German forces pressed on. From Klepawicze, the Brońskis – all except Adam – had already been sent to St Petersburg. Long lines of carts and livestock were filing every day through Nowogródek. News, rumours, counter rumours were all anyone mentioned. Adam Broński was about to empty the great vats of the Klepawicze still; the *spiritus* and the grain would be given to the peasants. Adam himself would wait and join the retreating Russian army.

Uncle Nicholas was unequivocal. He was sending all his valuables east. He told Helena's mother to take her children with them. He himself could not leave his land.

So one morning in early September Helena and her mother, and her brother and sister, and Panna Konstancja and Tekla rose at dawn and gathered on the drive in front of the house. Uncle Nicholas stood on the steps. He was wearing a long overcoat and a pair of Berber slippers. He traced the sign of the cross over each child.

A train of wagons already stretched away into the avenue. All Druków's valuables, all the furs and goldplate, the Persian silk carpets, the Saxony china and Kiev ware, and the trunks and trunks of Moroccan leather books, joined the bedding and fodder for the journey east. The horses were fidgety. Uncle Nicholas's foresters ran up and down the line shouting to each other, checking the harnesses, finding space for the last few boxes.

In charge of this strange caravan, and its team of *parobcy* drivers, was Pan Rymszewicz, Uncle Nicholas's gamekeeper. He put his lips to a hunting-horn and gave two blasts: the first carts lurched forward.

They drove out of the avenue. To the right a mist clung to the river but the water-meadows were empty. The cattle had already left. Passing the church, they joined the main road and turned into the sun. A small hill rose above the road and the track to Klepawicze led up over it. Waiting on the crest of the hill, beneath a clutch of larches was Adam Broński, seated on a bay mare. He galloped down to meet the wagons.

Reining in his horse he slowed to a walk and touched his hat to Helena's mother. '*Dzień dobry*, Comtesse.'

Some of his own carts, he explained, with the silver, had also left that morning. Could they join theirs? They would be waiting at the Niemen. He rode alongside for a few minutes, then trotted up to Helena: 'Good morning, Hela.'

'Good morning.'

There was silence between them.

'Panna Hela, you mustn't worry.'

'I am not afraid.'

'Are you sure?'

Helena nodded, looking across at him. He wore a peasant *czapka* with the peak pulled down to his forehead. She thought: what tiny kind eyes he has.

'Dobrze!' he cried suddenly and, reaching into his coat, pulled out a pocket-knife which he pressed into her hand. He was galloping back up the hill before she had a chance to thank him.

At noon they reached the Niemen. A narrow wooden bridge stretched across it and, while they waited for the Broński carts, Helena climbed down the mossy bank.

It was, she remembered, a hot and windless day. She stared into the water; the ink-blots of scattered clouds lay on the surface. Helena broke them with her fingers. She rolled up her sleeves and pushed her arms into the water. The water was cool and oily, and she splashed it on her face. No, she was not afraid. Quite the reverse. She was excited. She was overwhelmed by the familiar sense of something approaching.

She took out the pocket-knife and rinsed it; the haft was inlaid with mother-of-pearl and set into it, in silver, was a worn Broński crest. That a Broński should be capable of kindness, any kindness, was quite a shock to her.

Pan Rymszewicz's hunting-horn sounded and they carried on. They left the banks of the Niemen and plunged into dark forests where the sun slanted through the trees and the air was filled with the smell of pine resin. The noise of the convoy was louder among the trees, a noise of creaking axles, cracking reins and low voices.

At dusk they arrived in front of a small *dwór*. An elderly couple stood on the steps. Two ridgebacks jumped forward a few paces and then, seeing the size of the convoy, stood still and barked.

That night Helena ate in a vaulted dining room full of family portraits. She was given a room in the top of the house where the moon streamed over the boards and she slept deeply. At dawn Pan Rymszewicz's hunting-horn sounded out across the park and the whole convoy set off down a pale road that skirted the forest. They climbed and came out of the trees. Topping a low ridge, Helena saw the chalky ribbon of the road for miles ahead, meandering across the plain, splitting in two the brown smudges of small villages, dipping into hidden valleys, following the perimeter of a distant forest before burrowing into it.

The days fused one into the next. They travelled for one week, two weeks, a month. Sometimes they stopped for a few days before continuing their eastward trek. The forest banished all thought of war. Helena felt happy, exhilarated. Each day was different. Her mother withdrew the barbed constraints that normally surrounded her. She relaxed; the progress of the convoy imposed its own loose authority and, in years to come, Helena looked back on those weeks in the forest, seeing the horses' twitching ears, the arc of the wooden hames, hearing the creak of carts, and knew that this was the closest she ever came to any sort of freedom.

One night they stayed in a cabin on the summit of a small hill. All around them were camped the carts. Helena watched the fires stretch towards the trees. She left the cabin and walked through the camp. The smoke weaved up towards the great starry sweep of the Bird's Way. She felt like Queen Jadwiga wandering among her troops.

On another occasion, in late September, they passed through a village. An ox-cart blocked the road and, while waiting for it to be cleared, the Belorussian villagers gathered round the wagons. Their children were barefooted and the men had dirt in the lines of their faces. Pan Rymszewicz ordered them to clear the way but they pressed in closer.

He pulled his team off the road and led the convoy round towards the back of the village. He cracked a whip at two men who lunged for his reins. Others surged out of the crowd; one curled his stubby fingers around the calash hood of Helena's *bryczka*. He thrust his face in and for an instant she was staring into his eyes. She felt his breath on her face. He shouted something in a strange tongue and gripped her ankle. Then the horses leapt forward and he fell from the wagon, and they were bumping over the stony verge and into the fields.

After that Pan Rymszewicz avoided the villages. The convoy relied on the forest, and the hospitality of remote *dwóry*.

Some of the landowners were oblivious to the approaching Germans. The convoy arrived one afternoon at Wojopodorsk. The entire household was taking tea on the terrace, sitting at round tables, or on the steps, or standing importantly behind the chairs: old men in silk dressing gowns conferring, a boy with a pet rabbit, a widow with a dog in her lap, a young girl with her arm in a sling playing chess with a woman in a tiara of white lilac. The war, wrote Helena, was not mentioned at all by this family.

Others waited alone. They stayed once at a place called Barbarin, the home of a Graf Ignacy. A giant of a man, Graf Ignacy lived with his wife half a day's ride from the nearest town. In his dining room, dozens of elkheads stared down on a table with a worn, gold-threaded military saddle in the middle of it.

Helena watched him fill and re-fill his pewter plate with slabs of half-cooked roe deer; at his feet two red-toothed borzois pitted their jaws against its globular hip-joints.

'The Germans?' he spluttered. 'What do they know of the forest . . . We never budged for Bonaparte, why should we budge now?'

In the morning Helena heard gunfire; she opened the curtains and saw the cupola of Graf Ignacy's head thrust from a first-floor window; he was shooting rabbits on the lawn.

Many landowners had already left; sometimes Helena and the others spent the night on the bare boards of an abandoned house, and she would wake to sun in the curtainless windows and pick up her clothes and leave beneath huge chandeliers cocooned in dust-sheets.

In the first days of October, they arrived at Piesków, to the north-east of Minsk, home of Helena's uncle and a pair of very odd great-aunts.

The approach to Piesków, Helena recalled, was from below, over a little stone bridge with a wrought-iron fence on either side. Lilies lay on the lake below the bridge. The drive was made up of loose stones and gravel which crunched beneath the convoy's wheels. The carts pulled to a stop in a long line. On the steps stood a liveried butler and a fat man with a plum-red face. The butler was called Dominiecki; the red face was that of the land agent.

'Hrabina, Pani Hrabina!' Dominiecki stepped up to Helena's mother. He had a flustered manner. 'We heard of your coming, Hrabina. The Hrabia is fighting and the others have gone to Moscow only two days now. But we have instructions, Pani Hrabina, instructions. Please . . .' He bowed, clenching and unclenching his palms. Then he led them all into a hall with a vast, chess-board parquet floor.

After weeks in the forest Helena was shown up the wide stairs to a crisp-sheeted bed and a deep hip-bath. Lying back on the bed, she tugged off her boots; a shower of pine needles fell on the counterpane. She stepped barefoot to the window and watched the horses, bucking and kicking after harness, running around the paddock.

They spent a whole month at Piesków. The German offensive had slowed, and they had dug in to the west of Minsk. There would no more fighting, it was thought, until the mud had frozen and the roads were passable again.

Piesków was a strange household, and nothing was stranger than the two great-aunts who lived in the attic. Their presence hovered over the house like a taboo. The only approach to their rooms was a steep staircase and a door which was always closed. Sometimes they wouldn't come down for days and at these times their food was left on the stairs.

Helena remembered the older of the two – Aunt Minia – as an angry old woman with no time for anyone; what affection remained to her was directed towards two dozen rabbits which she kept in a fenced-off patch near the kitchen garden. If she talked at all, it was usually about rabbit manure.

Her sister was six foot six, deaf and famously holy. God had made her tall, people said, in order for her to be closer to Heaven. She spent her days, if not in the attic, in the Piesków chapel, her shoulders and long neck rising from the back pews like a steeple. Being deaf she rarely spoke; if she suspected someone of addressing her, she simply smiled and closed her eyes.

Helena sometimes glimpsed her in chapel, but never managed a word from her. Aunt Minia she talked to only once. Sitting in the corner of her rabbit hutch, the elderly woman was feeding lettuce leaves to an enormous jack rabbit. 'Who are you?' she asked.

'Helena.'

Aunt Minia gazed at her critically; the dog-sized beast munched away in her lap. 'What do you like doing?'

'Walking . . . riding. I read a lot.'

'Well, you're too pretty to be clever. Don't trust books and don't trust men with blue eyes or women who laugh. Stick to animals.' And the old woman slotted another leaf into the rabbit's mouth.

The land agent had a very frail wife who was also a distant cousin of Helena's mother. It was perfectly all right therefore for Helena to make friends with his daughters. Or one of them at least: the other, following an ill-starred liaison with a Russian officer, had attempted suicide and Helena was forbidden to talk to her.

The respectable daughter was called Zofia. She knew the forests well and the two of them spent much of their days riding, and swimming in the lakes.

After All Saints' Day came a spell of heavy rain and winds which filled the park with dancing leaves. Jews coming to buy calves whispered that the Germans had reached the Niemen. Other reports confirmed what they all feared: the advance was continuing.

Helena's mother summoned everyone, family and staff, to the hall. She said, 'The carts from Druków and Klepawicze must continue east. Whoever wishes to go with them may. But for the moment I am staying here.'

She then recited the '*Kto się w Opiekę*', 'Prayers to God's Providence', from Psalm 92:

> . . . *God will instruct His angels to attend*
> *Each of your movements*
> *And lead you, across the darkest place,*
> *The roughest place,*
> *Lest you bruise your foot against a stone* . . .

The next day a very worried Dominiecki rapped on the door of her room with word that a retreating Russian cavalry regiment had crossed the estate's marches.

'The officers are on their way here, Hrabina – to the house. What should I do?'

She opened the door. 'Welcome them, Dominiecki. They will give us news.'

'But they are not gentlefolk!'

'They are officers.'

'Yes, Pani Hrabina – but Russians!'

Late in the afternoon, a group of six hussars crossed the hall in shiny black boots. Helena's mother stood stiffly on the bottom stair. The colonel, an elderly Muscovite prince with drooping cheeks, kissed her hand. He greeted her in Parisian French and introduced his officers.

They spent the evening in the Piesków drawing room. When Helena crept in, hoping not to be noticed, the hussars sprang to their feet. They called her to the piano, 'Venez, Mademoiselle. On chante les chansons Russes!'

Helena's mother relaxed for the first time in weeks. She asked Dominiecki to bring some vodka from the cellar. Dominiecki looked grave: Russians in the house was one thing, but giving them vodka, that seemed to him very unwise.

At the end of the evening, the colonel took Helena's mother aside. 'I would urge you strongly to leave this house. Another offensive is underway.'

'An offensive?'

'The front is very close, Comtesse. It is a matter of days. It would be safer for you in Minsk, or better still, in St Petersburg.'

The next morning Helena's mother took her charges off again. The land agent sent his daughters with them.

Pulling out of the tracks of the estate, they joined the Minsk road. The mud was appalling. Helena described the scene: Russian soldiers and their carts and guns; many wounded; others with no more than bast sandals on their feet. She remembered a group of them leaning against the back of a clogged *tachanka*. They were trying to free it and, as she passed, she saw inside the *tachanka* a man lodged against a machine-gun. He looked at her blankly. He had lost both his legs.

After that the next few days blurred together. Helena wrote:

> . . . how I reached St Petersburg I can't remember. I remember the first day, travelling through the infantry column; I remember their grey faces and the Red Cross calashes. I remember the mud and the rain and the *dwór* with a gallery of silks and rolls of carpets in the hall. I remember the bodies in every room and someone whispering, 'No, Panna, not wounded – it's fever.'
>
> And that was all. Three days later we reached Minsk. My temperature rose on the evening of the first day. Tekla said it was typhus. They managed to keep me dry and somehow we reached Minsk. Where we stayed I don't know but one day, by chance, Mama saw Uncle Nicholas's brother on the streets. He had come down

from St Petersburg especially to find us. He was a wonderful kind man, a priest at that time, and he found us a place on a train to St Petersburg. No one thought I would survive the journey. The train was packed with hundreds of refugees like us, everywhere people ill and many died. The train stopped each morning for the bodies to be taken off. One of the people on the train was a famous surgeon and a friend of Uncle the Priest. Mama said that each day of that journey he came and saw me and gave me medicine. That man saved my life.

10

HELENA SPENT the greater part of two years in St Petersburg. Of this time she wrote later: 'these were in many ways the happiest years of my life. I came of age in St Petersburg, just as the city itself collapsed into chaos. I had never seen such splendour nor have I since . . .'

She was seventeen when she arrived, naive, private, used to the Kresy forests and the provincial life of Wilno. No photographs survive of her at this age, but in her notebooks of St Petersburg, written later, she drew an ink portrait of how she remembered herself, a neat and straight-backed girl dressed in fur, with a fur muff and a fur hat.

In St Petersburg too she had her hair cut short – so that it touched the bottom of her neck – and kept it like that throughout her adult life. She wrote that she learnt to 'wear clothes properly', choosing subdued colours and the 'classical lines' her father had wanted. It is clear that she was already beautiful, clear too that she was usually oblivious to the impression she was making – until it was too late. Things still happened *to* her. But St Petersburg opened her eyes.

Uncle Augustus – Uncle the Priest – found them a flat in a tenement off Ulitsa Pestelya. The panelled walls were varnished a deep burgundy red, the paintwork was white and the flat was very small – four rooms for Helena, her mother, her sister, the land agent's daughters, Panna Konstancja, and Tekla who slept in a broom cupboard off the kitchen.

Helena shared a room with her sister. It looked out over a dirty courtyard. At night the courtyard filled with cats that fought and screamed in the darkness. By day a second-hand light seeped down its high, chimney-like shaft. For the first months Helena was ill; she hardly left her room. From her bed she watched the snow-flakes corkscrew out of a grey sky. The days sped past and shrank. The doctor came with tonics of almond juice. Much of the time she slept.

On Christmas Day, 1915, Uncle Augustus stepped into the flat with a small Chinese song-bird in a cage. The bird had white feathers and a red bill. He hung him up in Helena's room and she christened him Liki. For a year and a half Liki trilled in his brass cage by the window. He hopped between his perches; he pecked at the sunflower seeds Helena fed him. Then came the revolution and Liki vanished. Never again did she hear the sound of passerine song without thinking of three things: the cardboard glamour of St Petersburg, the cry of fighting cats, and the sight of her father, leaning on an ivory-topped stick, on the corner of Nevsky Prospekt.

In the new year of 1916, Helena grew stronger. She was able to eat boiled vegetables and an occasional herring. The doctor moved her off almond juice and on to a special butter supplied to him direct from central Russia.

Late January brought frosty skies and a string of Polish émigrée women to the flat. They wore sable furs and big jewels to compensate for the loss of their estates. Their husbands were either fighting, or already dead. They failed to conceal their discomfort at the size of the O'Breifne rooms. They asked prying questions about food, laundry, and servants, and leaned around Helena's door to inspect her.

One of these women was Pani Józefina Pawłowska, 'a famous beauty', according to Helena. She arrived one day in an ankle-length zibeline coat. Standing for a moment by Helena's bed, she stretched out her hands and half closed her eyes.

'Blue – I see a blue aura around you!'

She sat down, crossed her legs, and tugged at the fingers of her black gloves. 'I have heard something of you from your mother. But she said nothing of your beauty. Wretched woman! A bit of flesh back on you, and you will be exceptionally pretty. Helenka, I believe I love you already! When you're better, promise to write and I will send my driver.'

By the beginning of February, Helena was almost fully recovered. Whenever the doctor brought his muslin bag of butter, she begged him to let her go out. On one day in February he turned to her mother and said, 'Ça va! La jeune fille va bien.'

A week later, a sled pulled up in the courtyard and took Helena off to the Pawłowski house on the Moika canal. She climbed down and looked at the building. It was more a small palace than a house. The walls were a pale green, with a colonnade of fluted pilasters between the windows. A large cupola, patinaed and guano-stained, stood on top.

Pani Józefina was sewing in her emerald-green boudoir.

'Hela,' she stood and kissed her, 'you look a hundred times better.'

'Thank you, Pani Józefina—'

'No! I am Aunt Ziuta to you.'

'Yes, Aunt Ziuta.' Helena perched on a cane chair.

'Do you feel better?'

Helena nodded.

Aunt Ziuta smiled her frightening half smile. She wore a white silk shirt and a grey pleated skirt. Everything about her was crisp and elegant; she spoke in the best Warsaw Polish. She was unused to being interrupted.

'Now, I want to know all about you. I imagine you understand nothing of life at all. That mother of yours! I suppose she taught you a few good prayers and told you to beware of men. Am I right?'

Helena nodded.

'Well, seeing that you are here in St Petersburg, you will be my charge. You will be part of my family. With me you will come to know life.' This last word she gave a peculiar, ambiguous emphasis. Then she smiled. 'And in exchange, I need your help.'

'Help, Aunt Ziuta?'

She smiled, running a hand down her swan-like neck. 'You will come to know, Hela, that for me there is only one thing worth living for, and that is music. My eldest son has a voice like an angel, a bass voice that can break your heart. He is six foot six and quite maddening. He thinks he is a socialist. He goes round all his father's factories preaching to the workers. They all think he's mad. He never sings now. Our musical evenings were famous but now he has no time for them. That is where you come in – do you see?'

Helena shook her head.

'Of course – you know nothing of men. But I guarantee that if you start to visit us, he will stay at home and stare at you and sing until he is quite hoarse.

'As for the rest of my household they are of little interest. With my husband it is all business, business, business. You will no doubt find Florian my younger son quite handsome with his great calf eyes. But he wastes his time with books of science. He is completely tone deaf.'

'Hela, *kochana*!' Aunt Ziuta greeted Helena on her second visit to the house. She led Helena through a series of rooms full of cut flowers, to a library and a long ballroom. At the far end of these cavernous rooms was a study. There, hunched over an oak desk, was the great Pan Pawłowski.

When Aunt Ziuta had married this man, in Warsaw, it was widely considered a *mésalliance*. He had, Helena recalled, brusque manners and was stout and rather animal in his ways. It was said his grandfather had been a Poznan peasant. But he proved a brilliant financier and built up a string of Russian factories. He amassed a fortune. In St Petersburg his baser quirks were accommodated: 'Ce cher Pawlowski est tellement original. C'est un original – enfin!' And in his deep armchairs and sofas, ambassadors and whiskered grand dukes came to exchange confidences.

When Helena entered his study, Pan Pawlowski stood and took both of her hands in his. He stared at her and said, 'You have great beauty, my girl. What will you do with it?'

'I want to study at university.'

He shook his head and laughed. 'No, no. I think not! Girls like you don't go to university!'

Helena said nothing.

Later she met his two sons. They made an odd pair. The one, Waldemar, tall, with dark hair, bowed as he took her hand; the other, Florian, a good foot shorter with huge grey eyes, stared at her in a disconcerting way.

That spring, Helena found her life dominated by the commanding figure of Aunt Ziuta. She spent a great deal of time at the Pawlowski house. She was invited to all the musical evenings and, sure enough, Waldemar began to have less time for politics and more time for singing.

Sometimes, on crepuscular afternoons, Aunt Ziuta would come to collect Helena and take her driving around the city, in a sleigh to begin with and then, in March, in an old and over-decorated carriage. The sun crouched on the skyline; St Petersburg rested on its swamp. It floated like a ship, and its orange façades, its lemon-yellow façades, its lime-green façades, its icing-sugar domes, seemed to Helena no more than players in some bizarre costume drama.

This was life, she thought. This was what Aunt Ziuta meant. She had only ever seen Wilno and Cracow and Warsaw, but St Petersburg and its people seemed altogether on a different scale. The town and the Pawlowskis became associated in her mind: St Petersburg was as appealing, and as heartless, as Aunt Ziuta herself.

They watched the guards goose-step at the Winter Palace; they saw Peter the Great rearing on his bronze horse. Aunt Ziuta had some colourful views on Russian history, and told Helena all the best anecdotes and scandals. She led her through the lit-up shops of Moskovsky Prospekt; they bought chocolates, tried on hats and furs and shoes. On the pavements of Nevsky Prospekt, Aunt Ziuta pointed out the ambassadors' wives, the generals, the Duma socialists. Once they saw Rasputin, reeling out of a carriage.

In late February Aunt Ziuta asked Helena and her mother to a gala performance of *Swan Lake* at the Mariinsky Theatre. The evening was sharp and frosty. Ranges of snow rose at each corner. Everyone seemed to be converging on the theatre entrance. Kozlinski, a favourite of the Tsar, was dancing the lead.

Helena remembered nothing of the ballet itself – only a semicircle of grand dukes, in white guards uniforms, standing on a red carpet in the foyer. That Tsar Nicholas himself stood in the middle of them. Helena hardly noticed. The grand dukes towered over him. They were like immortals, a medalled pantheon, creatures of another world. But it was the sight of Prince Yusupov among them (who later killed Rasputin) that stayed with her. 'Never have I seen such a beautiful man,' she wrote later. 'God broke the mould when he'd made Yusupov.'

On Saturdays there were dances at the Pawłowskis'. One of these, shortly before Lent, Aunt Ziuta elevated to a ball. It was Pan Pawłowski's birthday. To open the evening, Waldemar was persuaded to sing some arias of Mozart to please his mother, and then, to please his father, Polish folk songs to a balalaika.

Afterwards, with perspiration gleaming on his forehead, he came up to Helena.

'Bravo!' she said. 'Your father was delighted.'

'I care nothing for him. I sang for you only, Helenka.'

'Oh Waldemar, what idiocy!'

Later she danced with him – a polka – the first time she had ever danced at a ball. After it she sought out her mother. She found her in Aunt Ziuta's day-room, fanning herself among a group of Polish women.

'Mama! You missed the dance. I danced with Waldemar – you missed it!'

'Did you enjoy it, dear?'

'Oh, yes!'

'Well, you're not to dance with him again.'

The evening continued. Aunt Ziuta sat in front of the musicians, flanked by a pair of young hussars. A smile creased her cold face. Before her, the men of the Corps des Pages whirled around the floor. With their chiffoned partners, they danced polkas and quadrilles, an écossaise and a pas de chale. The head of Waldemar could be seen bobbing over the top of the Russians. Once or twice Pan Pawłowski crossed the ballroom, oblivious to all around him, hands clasped behind his back, deep in discussion with some minister or other.

For Helena, the high spot of the evening was returning home. Moonlit St Petersburg lay before her; the roofs white with hoarfrost, the river Neva nudging its cargo of ice-floes into the Finnish Straits. Beneath the furs, still dizzy from dancing, Helena listened to the swish of the skis and thought, 'How good to be alone again!'

One evening shortly afterwards, Aunt Ziuta took her aside. 'Hela, I don't know what the matter is. Half Petersburg is in love with you and you don't take a blind bit of notice! Look at your clothes. Are you ashamed of your looks?'

'No.' But she knew she was.

'What are you afraid of?'

'I don't know.'

'Are you afraid of me?'

'No, not you,' she said.

'Your mother?'

'Perhaps.'

'And that wretched Church of yours, no doubt! Look, Helenka, you must learn to be reckless.'

'Reckless?'

'Learn to wear your beauty like a joke. The more you treat it with levity, the more men will adore you. Always remember that men are like dogs.'

Suddenly Helena knew that she was wrong. 'But, Aunt Ziuta, I love dogs! More than anything!'

'Exactly,' she said, and a slow smile spread across her face.

11

IN THE SPRING OF 1916, news of the war reached
St Petersburg like sudden changes in the weather, sometimes
good, sometimes bad, always a surprise. The German advance
had slowed through the winter, but they were now well estab-
lished in Wilno. Helena's father, Count O'Breifne, had had no
leave. His regiment was based in Smolensk, and his letters
spoke of mud and epidemics, and the wolves digging bodies
from shallow graves.

One morning, early in the summer of 1916, Helena's mother
let out a small shriek. She dropped her newspaper. 'Dear Lord!
Stanisław Pawłowski has died!'

She went to telephone Aunt Ziuta. Helena picked up the
paper; there was no announcement of his death. And when
her mother returned, she looked puzzled. 'Stanisław himself
answered the telephone . . .'

Three days later Pan Pawłowski suffered a massive heart
attack; he died instantly. His funeral took place in St Catherine's
church on Nevsky Prospekt. The coffin was made of polished
ebony and wrapped with gold galloons. Aunt Ziuta stood beside
it in a thick mantilla and a long black coat. Not once during
the whole service did she move. When for the prayers the vast
congregation rustled to its knees, she remained standing. She
stared ahead as if carved from marble: the statue, thought
Helena, of some mythical apiarist.

In the weeks that followed Helena spent even more time
with the Pawłowskis. To begin with, death paralysed the household. The young daughter, Maria, hardly ate and would faint

frequently on the dozens of chintz sofas around the house. Florian paced the ballroom, holding his head. Aunt Ziuta received no one. Sitting straight-backed at the piano, she filled the house with the bom-bom-bom of Chopin's 'Funeral March'.

Meanwhile Waldemar renounced his socialism. Summoning his father's factory managers he told them, one by one, that he was taking over. Florian adopted his role as Helena's chief suitor and, when he was not filling notebooks with mathematical jottings, followed her every move with his big bovine eyes.

One afternoon in mid May she arrived at the Pawłowski home to find Aunt Ziuta playing Schubert's 'Impromptus'. Her widow's weeds were gone and she wore a yellow dress. The sun was bright through the open windows; coils of wisteria hung down the walls.

Aunt Ziuta stood and smiled. 'This evening Waldemar has agreed to sing, and a marvellous friend of his, a violinist, has just arrived from Moscow.'

Helena never heard Pan Pawłowski mentioned again.

The violinist turned out to be Helena's cousin, Andrzej Mostowski. She hadn't seen him since Wilno, where he used to chaperone her at dance classes. He wore a thin, meshy little moustache and was waiting to go into the army. She was overjoyed to see him.

To Andrzej, Helena was changed. 'All that running through the forest has made a woman of you!' he teased.

'Nonsense, Andrzej!'

'No, it's true.'

And she knew he was right. During the warm months that followed, she sensed a strange ease within her. She moved through those great rooms on the Moika canal, making light of the dragoons and their gangish attentions, of the leering landowners and the covetous industrialists; she danced and debated, heard extraordinary things about peasant Russia, about the war, about people with names from history books. She learned a little recklessness.

And she knew Andrzej was right when, turning over these evenings on slow drives home along the Neva, with a daylight blue filling the night sky, she could pick out all the prejudices and deceits of Aunt Ziuta's circle.

Yet when it came to herself, by her own admission, she was still as green as a spring beech.

One Sunday afternoon, she recalled, she sat in the Pawłowski drawing room with a young Estonian baron – a Lutheran named Lex Gintze. Lex was playing the piano. Helena was thinking about distant things.

Suddenly Lex let his fingers fall from the keys and turned to her. 'Panna Helena!'

'Yes.'

'You have beautiful legs!'

'What . . .'

'Beautiful legs, Hela!'

'Lex, what madness! How can legs be beautiful?'

But within a month Lutheran Lex, promising to become a Catholic, let it be known that he wanted to marry her. Helena was horrified. Her mother told him politely to wait, and taking Helena aside, chastised her for encouraging him.

Meanwhile there was good news from the war. On the Polish front, Brusilov had managed to push through the German lines; and for a few weeks the grumbling subsided.

Helena saw her cousin Andrzej frequently. They met at the Pawłowskis', at the musical evenings which continued throughout the summer.

Florian was now more intense than ever, and would take Helena away from the music, into the library to draw diagrams of the planets, or explain how a tree fed itself. Having completed his singing, Waldemar would then come in from the ballroom and rebuke his brother: 'Ach, Florian! Stop bothering poor

Helena! She's just not interested in all your wretched science!'

Sitting on her other side, Waldemar would then tell her about the danger of unions, about new shifts he had devised at his cabinet workshops, at an armaments factory, and the savings he'd made.

Andrzej was the only relief. He would come in, put down his violin and give a perfect imitation of the guests, the generals, the statesmen, all the men who had edged closer to Aunt Ziuta since the death of Pan Pawłowski. He was particularly good on a certain Italian count with his stock of badly sung arias. 'Now, look! He is crawling to her on his knees, like this: "Your eyes like jewels, darrleeng! Oh my 'eart, he is a furnace . . ."'

Helena became close to Andrzej; he was the first man she could talk to. He was the first man she liked being with, whose attentions did not make her feel ill. Perhaps, she wrote, she even loved him.

During July and August the O'Breifnes went to the Pawłowskis' dacha. The dacha was in a village near Terioki in Finland. Set amidst interminable forests, the village was little more than a long row of wooden cottages and smoky-grey birch trees. A group of larger houses had been built at the far end and one of these was the Pawłowskis'.

The paths of the village were spongy with moss. Long-limbed Finns wandered among them. They were pale-faced and taciturn. They clutched axes. But nothing ever happened in that village; it was a place of idyllic calm and it made Helena strangely uneasy.

Each morning, she walked to the Lutheran church, a tiny wooden building which smelt of dust and camphor. Helena, who always wore a dark velvet jacket, sat to one side. The services were conducted by a white-bearded priest and his pious son, Peter. Staring over the rim of the chalice, beneath a straw-blond fringe, Peter would raise his straw-blond eyebrows to

Helena and urge her to take the sacrament. She became used to dipping her gaze.

But one afternoon there was a knock on her door and she found Peter standing on the step. He held a bunch of forget-me-nots. He had put on a grey suit and a bright blue tie. Asking God to forgive him, he said in English, 'Miss Helena, you are the most woman I have seen. Please come walking on me!'

She thought it only fair to stop going to church.

Helena was working for exams. In October, she was due to sit for a diploma in English, and a Miss Gardner came up from St Petersburg to give her lessons.

Miss Gardner was a lonely, peripatetic young Londoner whom Uncle the Priest had just received into the Catholic Church. She was only twenty-two; she had long fair hair plaited like bandages around her head, and wore green blouses and amber beads. Helena found her lessons very tedious. She reminded her of her mother, and this always put her off.

'Now, repeat after me,' said Miss Gardner, '"From her unhasty mule she did descend, and on the grass her dainty limbs did lay . . ."'

Helena repeated the verses, but in truth her attentions were elsewhere – back in St Petersburg, back in the linden avenues of Wilno, back with Andrzej. The jagged forest skyline beyond the window became more familiar to her than anything by Wordsworth or Spenser or Chaucer.

Helena fell into a mid-summer torpor. For company of her own age she had only Maria Pawłowski. Florian was there too but behaving very strangely, even for him. He rose long before anyone else and would stumble in through the front door at breakfast, his eyes restless, his coat studded with thorns.

He wouldn't eat, and Aunt Ziuta gave up with him.

One evening Helena was picking flowers some way into the forest. The shadows were heavy across the path. In the top fringes of the pines, clouds of midges spiralled against a blue sky; finches sang in the treetops. Resinous smells thickened in the summer air.

Helena was idly murmuring to herself in English, '. . . And on the grass her dainty limbs did lay . . . and on the grass her dinty dibs did lay . . . and on the path the stupid *anglais pays* . . . and on the grass . . .'

Bending to pick an orchid, she saw a figure wandering through the trees. It was Florian. He saw her and came over. He said nothing. His temples were sweaty and his eyes wide. He stood there panting like a dog, then reached out for Helena. She dropped her flowers and ran back to the village.

A few days later, in the second week of August, Waldemar came up to the dacha with Andrzej, and Helena's days brightened up. Andrzej had just joined the Corps des Pages, and made everyone laugh with his imitation of the Russian officers.

At about noon each day, they would pack a pony with food and walk through the forest to the sea. There was a place there with a short jetty where you could swim.

Helena, Waldemar and Florian sat above the shore, perched on the lip of soil that overhung the rocks. Andrzej was swimming, and a cool wind blew in off the water.

'St Petersburg is changing,' said Waldemar.

Helena looked across at him. 'What has been happening?'

'Meetings, these meetings. No one is happy with the war. Constant talk against the empress and Rasputin. Last week I had to dismiss three of my managers for organizing a union.'

Florian scoffed at his brother. 'A year ago, you were organizing the unions yourself!'

'You understand nothing, Florian.'

'Hypocrite!'

'What do you know of real life? Eh? You just fill your head with the planets and your pointless sums . . .'

Florian's doe eyes narrowed; he stood up clumsily. He glared at Waldemar, at Helena, then disappeared into the forest. No one saw him again that day.

The next morning was bright and cool. The dew lay thickly around the house. Helena went out after breakfast, sticking to the road to keep her shoes dry. In the meadows the grass was hung with gossamer threads; the early sun made them shine like water.

A little way beyond the houses, she came across Florian. He smiled and greeted her with a faint bow. 'Panna Helena.'

He seemed calm and Helena felt strangely sorry for him. She wanted to help. 'What is the matter, Florian?'

He shook his head.

'Something is the matter. Tell me.'

He broke a dead branch from a larch. She watched him snap it in two; then he snapped the two pieces into four, and continued to snap them until they were all too small to snap any more. He threw them away.

'What is it, Florian?' she repeated.

'It's you, Hela.'

She said nothing.

'I love you.'

'No, please!'

'I want to marry you.'

'No!'

'Why not?' He stared at her fiercely.

'Just no.'

'Is it Andrzej? Would you marry Andrzej?'

'I don't know. He hasn't asked me.'

'But if he asked you?'

Helena shrugged. 'Perhaps.'

Florian stopped suddenly on the road. He clenched and unclenched his fists, then stood staring at his palms.

Helena turned on her heels and left him. It was time for Miss Gardner.

Later that morning one of the Finns found Florian in a patch of fern beyond the village. There were mushrooms in the grass beside him. Andrzej's service revolver was in his right hand; the barrel was in his mouth.

Above his body the bracken was just beginning to turn autumnal brown.

In her account, Helena says nothing about her reaction to Florian's suicide. She simply said that the first thing Aunt Ziuta – his mother – did was to embrace her, saying, 'It was not your fault, my darling, and anyone who says it is will have to deal with me.'

She looked to Andrzej for solace, but they both realized it had changed. Even back in St Petersburg it was different. The silences between them were shadowy and taut. Florian was always there, just as he had been in life.

12

IN THE AUTUMN OF 1916 there were many strikes. The gates of the Petersburg foundries and wool mills were often locked. Groups of workers gathered outside them, their hands stretched over braziers. Near the docks certain men stood on upturned fish-crates and talked of things that few in their audience seemed to understand. The days grew shorter; the speeches grew longer.

Sometimes there were bands of mounted policemen posted around the city. They held long pikes and wore greatcoats which flared out over their saddles. The horses stamped impatiently and breath steamed from their nostrils. In her account, Helena confessed that she was oblivious to the mounting tension. But she always noticed the horses.

She had passed her exams with distinction. The directors of the English school – an odd pair known as Miss Sanders and Mr Pike – said that during the war it was not possible to get teachers from England, as was their policy, but could she take a class?

'Helping to spread the lovely language of Shakespeare,' sighed Miss Sanders. 'Surely one of the noblest things a young person can do.' And Helena was flattered enough to agree.

So at 5 p.m. the following Monday, in a grey cardigan, she pushed open a frosted glass door marked 'FORM IV – Berkshire (Only English spoken)'. A row of staring Russian eyes greeted her. She had been given a class of twenty-three civil servants.

She introduced herself in English. The eyes stared.

She stood in front of the blackboard and placed her hands on the back of her chair. 'What is this?'

The eyes blinked.

'This is: *a chair.*'

'*A sheer* . . . *a cheer* . . . *a jair* . . .'

The first lesson was a sticky affair. None of the class had a word of English and Helena was shy. She had never been alone in a room with so many men before.

But in the following weeks they made more progress. The clerks proved keen and good-humoured. Helena became fond of them and sometimes the hour-long evening lessons would stretch to two, even three hours. Soon they were reading Aesop's *Fables* and conducting faltering debates about goats and lions and birds. The snow built up in arcs across the windows, muffling the sounds from the street.

Perhaps, thought Helena, Miss Sanders was right. She made plans to become a teacher, to help 'spread the lovely language of Shakespeare'.

In St Petersburg, the O'Breifnes had very little money. Their life was frugal and plain and Helena resented it. On receiving her first pay she said to her mother, 'Enough of these economies!' and went to Gostinny Dvor and bought her a new watch. It was a barbed gift. Relations between mother and daughter deteriorated step by step. One Sunday afternoon Helena's mother found her complaining to Andrzej on the telephone. Snatching the receiver from her hand, she cried, 'Telephoning men is the habit of seamstresses!'

Helena turned in anger. 'Mama, he said something . . . Andrzej said he saw Papa. Why didn't I know? Why isn't he here, staying with us?'

'It is not your business. He is ill.'

'He is my father! I want to see him.'

'I will not allow it.'

But from Aunt Ziuta, Helena found out that he had taken a small flat on Nevsky Prospekt. She went there at once.

Uncleared snow lay in the courtyard. She climbed the stairs and when he opened the door had to make an effort to greet him normally. He looked very ill. His face was drawn and sallow-skinned; his uniform sagged on his shoulders and on his hips. He had black smudges under his eyes, yet oddly he seemed younger. He pointed Helena to a desk chair, and sat down opposite her.

'Hela, my dear Hela!' He leaned forward and took her hand. 'You are grown up, Helenka. You must see that your mother and I do not get on.'

'But why, Papa?'

'She made me promise never to see the woman you call Aunt Janienka. I could not promise such a thing, so she does not want me. She has no use for me any more.'

'How can I see you? I must see you!'

He held up his hands and smiled. 'All right, Hela, here's what we'll do. I will come for you each evening at the English school, and we will walk here and have supper in my room and afterwards I will take you home. Tell your mother you eat at the school and no one will ask questions.'

So every evening he was there sitting on a wooden bench in the hall of the English school, waiting for Helena's class to finish. And the rumour began, among the grinning Russian clerks and the thinly scattered staff, that this man, this dashing man of forty-eight, was really her fiancé.

She did nothing to deny it. She called him 'Józef' in their presence. He in turn took to arriving with gifts of chocolates and flowers; sometimes he donned his uniform and Miss Sanders whispered to Helena, 'Such a handsome man. 1917 will be your year, Miss O'Breifne, I know it! A lovely spring wedding!'

Mr Pike put an avuncular arm around her shoulder and warned her about men who were 'philanderers and black-guards'.

But all the while Helena's father was getting weaker. At Christmas there was a party in the flat and he came and sat in a corner. Twenty people filled that flat. They picked at a pair of geese that Tekla had found from somewhere. There were noisy toasts and noisy Polish singing.

During the height of the party, Helena looked around and saw that her father was missing. She went into the back of the flat and found him in her own room. He was sitting on her bed, leaning over a bucket and vomiting. He tried to laugh it off: 'The doctors, Hela, they say my stomach is narrowing. The solution is simple – all I must do is eat less!'

'History', Aunt Ziuta had said once, on one of those summer evenings on the Moika canal, 'is like a hare waiting in the bushes.'

Now it was winter. The Moika canal was frozen. St Petersburg was ploughing through the icy wastes of the new year. The sun shone yellow on the underside of the clouds. Sometimes there was a wind and it blew fiercely across the empty squares, searching the streets for loose snow. Sleighs slid to and fro, reluctant to stop; no one went out to shop as there was nothing to buy. The Neva, where only a month or so before Rasputin had been jammed through the ice, stretched like a white no man's land through the city. Mounted police barred the bridges across it; distant shouting echoed off the river. The hare waited in the bushes.

In February Helena's English classes grew smaller. They were reading Kingsley's *The Water Babies*, and the twenty-three grinning clerks became twenty, then fifteen, then ten. There was shooting on Nevsky Prospekt and then only five appeared; and one day after a heavy snowfall, with the streets full of troop carriers, only Ivankienko, an earnest Russian from the Urals, managed to get through. He pulled from his coat a pot of raspberry jam, and gave it to Helena. 'Oh

Miss! For you the jam! You must not go to hunger . . .'

At that moment, the main door opened. Helena's father stood breathless on the threshold. 'Quick, Hela . . . Fighting has broken out . . .'

Outside, there was the sound of gunfire. Groups of men were running through the streets; some were clutching shards of ice from the canal.

The three of them hurried out of the school. They crossed open squares, passed boarded shops and iced-up trams; they made progress street by street, doorway by doorway. Helena's long skirt became stiff with snow and swung like a bell against her felt boots. The cold tore at the back of her throat.

'Quick!' coaxed her father. But he too was in pain. He gripped his side. Ivankienko ran ahead, checking at each corner for barricades, the pot of raspberry jam clutched tight against his chest.

On a bridge over the Griboyedov canal, three men were standing on a dray cart. They were addressing a small crowd of workers and soldiers with rifles. Some were firing into the air. Ivankienko put an arm in front of Helena and halted her. They retraced their steps.

Around the back of Gostinny Dvor, they stumbled across a group holding red banners. Someone was signing the 'Marseillaise'. Ivankienko pressed Helena into a doorway. The men were standing in a semi-circle. They were shouting at a police officer; the officer was on horseback. He was trying to spur himself away, but they closed in around him. One of the group had the reins and the others were tugging him from the saddle. The officer fell. He tried to run away, but they pushed him to the ground. One of the crowd took a lump of ice, about the size of his fist, and started beating it against the man's head. His head flopped forward. Someone held it back by the hair. They carried on beating him until he was dead.

Helena never forgot that scene; she never forgot the look in his eyes, nor his blood in the snow. It was the moment, for her, when the world finally lost its innocence.

For some time the city was in chaos. Helena didn't go out, not even to see her father. Tekla would come in after hours of foraging with only a loaf or a few pickled vegetables to show for it. She fed them the latest rumours – that the Volhyn Regiment had mutinied, that Khabalov was mounting a counter-attack, that the Corps des Pages were defending the Winter Palace, that the Tsar was far away; that the Tsar had abdicated.

And then a kind of order returned. The trams and buses ran again and a little food found its way into the shops. Helena resumed her classes and her clerks came back, one by one, looking thinner, with tighter grins, until the class was twenty-three again. They finished *The Water Babies*, and moved on to Kipling.

One afternoon – it was a Saturday and the lime trees were a hazy green – Helena walked home across the Mars Fields. She remembered the dark clouds overhead and the rubbery squeak of the snow beneath her feet. She thrust her hands deep inside her coat. Across the expanse of the park, she could see a crowd gathered in the corner. A man was standing at the front on a wooden box. He was hatless and nonchalant in the cold. She drew closer and could make out his words:

'Every man is master of his destiny . . . He must shape his own destiny and help shape that of his country . . . Your time has come, people . . .'

Back at home she found Uncle Augustus standing in front of the Dutch stove.

'Uncle.' She stretched to kiss him, then started to take off her gloves. 'Such a curious man was speaking today in the Mars Fields. But what a beautiful voice he had! Such intelligence!'

'Who was he?'

'They said his name was Lenin.'

And the situation had not really improved. There were still men with brooding eyes everywhere, still shooting in the streets. Running to her father's flat with a flask of Tekla's vegetable bouillon, Helena frequently saw the bodies discarded like rubbish in the doorways.

Her father also remained in a state of uncomfortable limbo. Helena spent Sunday afternoons with him. When in pain, he would hold a towelling-wrapped samovar to his stomach. As the pain eased he slept. She watched him sleep. She listened to the French ormolu clock chiming away the hours. There was always a point when his hands dropped away from the samovar, his head slipped to one side, and the skin around his cheeks softened; then for a while he seemed at peace.

In April, Aunt Ziuta took Helena to a ballet at the Mariinsky. Even though the city was in flux, the auditorium was full, the performance flawless. To Helena it was much less of a spectacle without the silks and jewellery, without the archdukes, without Yusupov.

Afterwards, in the square, a *babushka* stepped out in front of them. She had blue eyes and grub-like fingers. One of these she thrust at Helena. 'I have a hat for you, my girl, a crepe mourning hat!' She put a piece of paper into Helena's hand.

Aunt Ziuta led Helena away. 'C'est rien. La femme est folle!'

Later Helena unravelled the bit of paper. There was an address on it, somewhere behind the theatre. She traced it, several days later, to the fourth floor of a soot-blackened house. A pipe was leaking in the hallway, and a stream of water dripped down the stairwell. The rooms were full of people on straw mattresses. She was about to leave when her *babushka* came hopping across a row of sleeping bodies, holding a hat.

'Your hat, Miss. I made it for you.'

'But I don't need a hat.'

'You will,' she laughed, and taking a clutch of coupons from Helena's hand left her with the hat.

Meanwhile her father grew worse. He could not hold down even Tekla's broth. The doctors decided to operate and on the 10 May – 27 April in the old calendar – he was taken to a large army hospital. Helena, her mother, Uncle Augustus and Panna Konstancja waited outside.

It was mid afternoon when the surgeon came out. He was smiling; the operation had been a success. Helena's father was wheeled out on a trolley, and they waited for him to wake.

Half an hour later, he opened his eyes. He tilted his head towards Helena and her mother, and smiled. Then he went back to sleep. Soon afterwards his eyes opened suddenly. This time he looked surprised. The professor rushed to his side. He took his wrist, leaned on his chest. He shouted for a nurse and they both pummelled his chest. Then the professor pursed his lips and pulled the sheet up over his patient's face.

Helena's mother stared at the trolley. She had seen it before in her dreams. She had seen it after his 'visits' in the early years of their marriage. These fleeting encounters used to fill her with such horror that she would become blind afterwards and the only thing that ever broke the darkness was this: the vision of her husband, harmless, lying on a table wrapped in a white shroud.

In Poland the custom was to take the dead home and make a *'Chapelle Ardente'* where family and friends could come and pray before the body was buried.

Helena wanted a *Chapelle Ardente* but her mother refused. 'These are dangerous times, dear. It's best to leave it.'

All the following day Helena stayed in the flat. She sat unpicking the stitches of a cushion; Liki chirruped over her head. By the evening, Panna Konstancja could take it no more. She took her aside and told her where her father was lying.

The *dvornik* swung open the oak door. It was 10 p.m. and very cold. She pulled a woollen scarf up around her mouth and hurried along the canal. There was no one else on the street.

What Helena remembered of this journey was hazy and disjointed. She followed the route mechanically. She crossed the Neva with the moon broken to pieces in the rippled water. There was then a white-bearded night-watchman who muttered amiably as he admitted her to a room of low vaults and simple altars hidden in the niches.

The room was full of corpses. They lay on stone plinths and tables; they lay between the tables, on planks and loose duckboards. Some were wrapped in sheets and sackcloth, but others were still in their clothes.

'Counter-revolutionaries!' whispered the old man.

Her father was on his own in a corner. He was wrapped in the same hospital sheet. She took a candle and sat with him and laid a hand on the sheet. She felt the calico warm and sticky against her skin. Her fingertips were covered in fresh blood. She jumped up. 'He bleeds! Look, he is alive!'

The watchman came over and shook his head. He left Helena with a clutch of candles, and she sat there all night. She slipped in and out of sleep. Then she slept properly and when she awoke the candles had burnt down and the shadows had receded. Dawn had entered that dank ward and her father's face was grey.

The attendants came down the stairs. They crossed to the basin; they chatted while scrubbing their forearms. They hauled the bodies off the plinths and on to stone slabs.

In a daze, Helena watched these corpses being washed. In a daze, she watched Tekla arrive and Panna Konstancja and Uncle Augustus who said Mass in one of those cave-like niches. She remained motionless on her stool, unable to focus on anything but the pale and beautiful face of Aunt Janienka bowed before the altar, the slow leonine way in which she moved: this woman who had taken her father away. It was the only time she ever saw her.

And then, wrote Helena, there was another great blank in her memory and there was nothing of the burial nor the last days in St Petersburg nor the goods train which hurried them away. There was only the image of herself, a listless figure back at Piesków, in black, too tired to take in a word of Dickens's *A Tale of Two Cities* which lay unread in her lap.

13

HELENA SPENT most of the summer of 1917 at Piesków, just to the north of Minsk. Of these days she recalled:

> When I think of that summer it is not the uncertainty nor the shock of our flight from Petersburg, nor even the gloom at my father's death. It is the sunny days, the columns of the old manor, the light falling through the forest, the sound of the stream at night, and the bench on which I sat listening to the passionate words of ecstasy and love, repeated over and over again, by the debonair and handsome Medeksa.

The arrival at Piesków marked the beginning of Helena's most turbulent years. Germans and Russians came and went; borders shifted like the tide, washing everyone up in different towns, in different countries. There were farm carts and forest drives and nights in Jewish inns. But something had changed. The journeys were different from the flight of 1915. That had been an adventure. Now the world was a darker place. Everyone Helena knew or loved was either scattered by the war, or dead.

Her mother, widowed, became harder. She took to drinking black coffee and smoking Turkish cigarettes. She was keen for Helena to marry, yet couldn't bear seeing her with men. Helena frequently promised herself to be rid of them all and live alone, without her family, without admirers, in some cabin in the forest, surrounded by dogs and horses and wild bees.

But Medeksa's words of ecstasy and love were very pleasant

– so pleasant that after several weeks of them, Helena became convinced she had committed some sin.

Medeksa was 'old' – more than twenty-eight. He had been serving in the Red Cross *Otryads* in the Bukovina and was now stationed in a field hospital near Piesków. He was widely read in English and French and when it came to talking of poetry – as it always did – he would quote great tracts from Baudelaire's *Fleurs du Mal*, or Rimbaud's *Une Saison en Enfer*. He knew that words alone were the key to Helena's heart.

In time, her mother found out. She was very angry.

Helena reassured her. 'It's all right, Mama . . .'

'What do you mean, "It's all right"? The man is untrustworthy!'

'I am going to marry him.'

'What?' She drew sharply on her cigarette. 'One does not marry doctors!'

Her mother's vehemence pushed Helena closer to Medeksa. He took to writing her long letters from his hospital, always headed with a couplet of French or English verse, and always scented with apple blossom.

Then in September her mother said they were moving to Minsk. It would be safer in Minsk, she said. Safer with Uncle Augustus.

He too had fled the increasing chaos of St Petersburg. He was now a bishop and had been given a large house near the cathedral in Minsk. It was a beautiful house, its outside walls feathered with creeper, its high rooms decked out in episcopal splendour. But in those dark days it felt oddly deserted. Helena had the sense that there was always someone missing, that they had pushed open the door and simply stepped inside.

They were constantly hungry. Everyone was hungry. That winter was even worse than the last. They would gather in the dining room knowing, as Uncle the Bishop said Grace, that all they were thanking God for, at best, was a few cubes of horseflesh.

Helena's grandmother was also with them. She was oblivious to most things and, humming quietly, spent her time sitting in the parlour stitching brown flannel shirts for the poor.

At the other end of the house lived a young curate, tall and thin like a poplar. He painted scenes from the life of Christ: great blocks of colour with twisted, scarecrow figures. Helena used to watch him work. She marvelled at the care that went into something which turned out so dull. He took her interest for admiration, and when he left, on a special mission to Rome, presented her with a picture of the disciples crossing a cornfield.

'How lovely,' she exclaimed. 'Boats, on a lovely yellow lake!'

Helena carried on her teaching. She gave classes in English to two 'dim-witted' Russian princesses. She discovered her lifelong intolerance of mediocrity. One evening in October, her princesses came to her in tears.

'Oh Helena! We have to leave, this evening!'

'Where to?'

'Away!' they said.

'Where away?'

'We don't know!'

'Well, why must you leave?'

'Oh Helena, we don't know!'

Typical of their answers, she thought.

But the reason was soon clear. Later that week, with the trees bare and all but the crows flown south, the Bolsheviks took control of Minsk.

Overnight the city changed. Men wearing red armbands filled the streets, spitting sunflower seeds into the gutters. The Bolshevik governor came to Uncle the Bishop and told him to leave. He refused, and one night they machine-gunned the cathedral windows. The following day every Pole in Minsk rallied round the building and the Bolsheviks, still unsure of their support, left them alone.

Uncle the Bishop mulled over the problem. He decided to

give a reception. He invited the Poles, and he invited the Bolshevik governor. No one expected him to come but he did, a youngish man with round glasses, attended by two commissars. They tried not to stare at the red silks of the women and their jewels, at the twelve-foot aspidistra in one corner, at the dusty authority shining from the room's portraits. They left early.

The party carried on long into the night. The toasts rambled, the singing grew louder, the dancing quicker. The curate fell behind a sofa. Helena was dancing with a distant cousin when she spotted Medeksa in the doorway. But before she managed to reach him, Uncle the Bishop had told him to leave.

The next day, at breakfast, a letter arrived and the dining room filled with the scent of apple blossom. Helena's mother took the letter, tore it up and scattered its pieces in the fire. 'That man is no good for you, Hela.'

All through that winter Helena laid plans to meet him; each of them came to nothing. The only time she ever saw him was at evening Mass, when he sat in a pew behind her, his eyes on her neck. But her mother was always with her and she could not talk. Anyway, she wrote, she was much too busy praying to take any notice.

Outside church, she became increasingly distracted. She stared at her books as if they were in Urdu. She met a kindly priest, Father Rostowski, who listened to her closely and then said, 'Love is like ivy, Panna Helena; it can grow through even the thickest wall.'

Father Rostowski took the case to heart. He saw Medeksa, and promised to help. He went with his dilemma to Uncle Augustus. But Uncle Augustus was his bishop and told him not to meddle; he accused him of behaving like a Bolshevik, a Trotsky of family affairs.

As for Helena, she remained more determined than ever. One afternoon, after a complicated series of letters sent through

Panna Konstancja, she left the house and met Medeksa by the river.

It was a bright winter's day. She wore a summer dress under a thick coat; he wore an orchid in his button-hole. They sat together on a bench. All around the park the grass was showing through ribbons of ice; tiny buds were visible on the trees. They talked of everything, of food and music, of St Petersburg and God, of the Bolsheviks and Verlaine. They laughed easily and Helena felt buoyant and happy. Then he ran his arm along the top of the bench and kissed her.

Helena leapt up. 'Medeksa!'

'What's the matter?'

'Do you take me for a housemaid?'

'My poor, poor Helena . . .'

'Don't "poor Helena"! I am not one of your nurses.'

'Oh, you and your snobberies! You're really no different from your mother!'

Helena turned and left, alarmed to discover that he was right.

The weeks passed and the Bolsheviks gained in strength. The streets became choked with soldiers in grey uniforms, the gutters with their sunflower seeds. They went about in pairs, gesticulating madly, peering through the windows of abandoned villas. Several times they pushed past Uncle the Bishop's butler and wandered in and out of the rooms. At night, friends disappeared. Uncle the Bishop's life was threatened. He placed a permanent guard on the churches and Helena's mother offered up her Prayers of Providence.

Providence knocked again. On the very day that the Red Guard was despatched to arrest the O'Breifnes, the Germans re-took Minsk. Prisoners were freed and for a time there was food.

German officers began to come to tea with Uncle Augustus;

he had been to a Jesuit seminary near Innsbruck, and spoke a good, high German.

One day they reported that there was a camp on the edge of Minsk, a refugee camp full of displaced Poles. Helena asked to see it.

'It is not something for young ladies,' said a major.

'That means it must be worth seeing, Herr Major.'

The following afternoon, flanked by the major and his aide-de-camp, Helena rode through the Minsk streets. There were parties clearing the streets of its war debris; there were sentries on the city fringes; Helena realized she hadn't been outside Minsk for nine months.

But then the skies blackened. A sudden breeze scooped up the dust from the empty road and the horses shied; thunder rolled in from the plain. When it started to rain, the ADC said above the noise of the wind, 'Miss Helena, we must turn back!'

Panna Konstancja came in the following day with a letter for Helena. The letter had no couplet, and no apple blossom:

> Panna Hela,
>   I thought that this love I have kept within me would not be wasted. I have heard nothing from you and now I see you riding with German officers. You and your family are not true Poles. The only decent one among you is your grandmother who visits the poor and the prisoners and is a great Polish patriot. If only you took after her . . .
>   Leave the Germans alone. Medeksa.

Helena threw the letter aside. She did not answer it. She wrote instead to the German major and repeated her intention to go to the camp at the first opportunity.

He came after two days. 'Fraulein,' he said, bowing slightly from the waist.

They rode out of Minsk on the Smolensk road. It had rained

in the night. A thundery heat pressed down on the land and the horses were jumpy. They splashed through the puddles; the reins left sweaty streaks on their necks. The major sat straight in his saddle, one hand on the pommel.

There wasn't very much on the road – no carts (the war had taken all the horses) and no cattle. The crops looked very thin and burdock and thistle grew among them.

After St Petersburg, Helena imagined she was used to destitution. She had seen the poor there and she had seen the dead. But it had not prepared her for that camp. Hundreds and hundreds of people were squatting in the mud. Their children lay bare-legged beside them. Babies were bundled to the women's breasts. Stooped figures shuffled about, collecting water from puddles. Illness hung over that place like the thunder-clouds. Everyone was ill – ill from dysentery, ill from typhus, ill and widowed from other people's war, other people's ideas, other people's revolution.

Helena said she felt a powerful urge to leave. She wanted to scrub her hands and sit in the window where the sun came in and read her books. But the impulse to stay was stronger. She could not take her eyes from that scene. She rode around the camp until a group of women surrounded her and tugged at her skirts and begged her for clothes and food.

She rode back in silence with the major. She felt dazed. Then she felt angry, then decisive. She would set up a committee! She would raise funds from all the wealthy Poles! Uncle Augustus will appeal to Rome! She herself would learn to nurse, would learn about dressings and dispensing and how to give vaccinations . . . and then she thought of Medeksa.

'I spent a whole day writing the letter,' she recorded. 'I told him of my plans; humbly, I confessed my faults; I talked of the timeless nobility of treating others: I told him I would like to grow old treating others as he did. I said that I loved him, that I didn't care what my family thought. I wrote the letter again and again, toning it down, toning it up, before sealing up the envelope and despatching it to his hospital.'

That evening she ate nothing. She knew that in effect she had committed herself to marrying Medeksa – if he was still interested. She looked around the table, at her mother and the bishop, at the long table and the silver and the portraits, and thought: this could be the last evening.

And so it was. At seven o'clock the next morning, there was a knock at the door. It was the German major. 'We have reports of a Bolshevik uprising. You must leave at once!'

Helena thought of staying, but seeing the speed with which her mother packed, she knew she must follow – just as she always had.

From the train she watched Minsk slide past the window; she watched the church towers and villas, the tramways and cobbles; she watched the town give way to low hills and the roads which wound into the distance. Then the train entered the forest and the trees blocked her vision. Helena never saw Minsk nor Medeksa again.

—————

14

IT WAS EARLY SUMMER 1918 when Helena and the
O'Breifnes arrived in Wilno. Minsk, Medeksa, St Petersburg,
Helena's father – countless towns and one-night stops – were
behind them. They brought nothing. They were refugees like
everyone else. They had been refugees since the day in 1915
when Helena had watched her grandmother's prize horses trotting up Mała Pohulanka, fleeing the Germans. That had been
in Wilno. They had now come full circle.

But still nothing was settled. The Bolsheviks were on the
move and the Germans were weakening. A swathe of unoccu-
pied and semi-occupied territory had opened up between them.
Wilno was in this territory.

They had been in Wilno only a few days when Helena's
mother announced they were leaving: for the *dwór* of some
great-aunt – a house with pompous, wine-red rooms and a
garden as bleak as snow. Then, after a week, they returned to
Wilno; there was talk of Warsaw, of Cracow, but in the end they
returned to the aunt's *dwór* where, wrote Helena, her mother 'sat
smoking all day in that tomb of a drawing room'.

A few weeks later, Helena began to hear mentioned the name
of Platków, home of her grandparents, the house where she had
been brought up, and with the name came the thought of all
her vanished pre-war certainties.

They left for Platków the following week. The journey, by
cart, took five hours. The house itself was very run-down.
Helena's grandparents had left it in 1915. Paint peeled from
the walls and in dozens of places the brickwork was exposed.

Szymon, who had been Platków's land-agent for as long as anyone could remember, was dead. So was his dog Zółtaik. The stables were empty. The pedigree horses were lost in Russia. Only Ewa stood on the step to greet them – Ewa the house-keeper, who had remained there throughout the war and was now widowed like everyone else. She stood waving with both hands. Beside her stood three German officers.

Platków had been requisitioned by the Wirtschafts Offiziese, responsible for collecting milk and eggs and grain from the villages for their troops. They were not pleased to see the carts.

Helena brushed past them and went inside, wandering from room to room. The valuables had gone – into Russia for safety in 1915 and now in Bolshevik hands. The rooms, many of them shuttered, looked like barrack rooms and smelt of unwashed men. She stepped out into the garden. The wind hissed among the birches and she wondered if there was anything anywhere that remained untouched by the war.

That evening, a man rode up the avenue on a bay stallion. Dismounting, he handed the reins to one of his officers and bowed. He introduced himself to Helena's mother as Freiherr von Sanden, District Commandant.

'Of course, Hrabina. You must reclaim your house. I will see my men are re-billeted.'

And with a click of the heels, Freiherr von Sanden was gone. He trotted off beneath the chestnut trees with his officers obediently following behind him.

At Platków, the days soon found their own rhythm. Helena, her mother and sister, Panna Konstancja and Tekla – the same five who had remained together throughout those three years – now felt in some way that they had returned.

But they were very isolated. They lived in a country that was not a country at all. No one was responsible for anything. The Germans ran what trains and post they needed, but no more.

'Like fishes,' Helena's mother said. 'We are like blind fishes swimming in a net.'

She allotted them all daily tasks. Each morning Helena had to fetch milk from the cottages, then boil up lye in old kettles to make soap; she made wheat starch with Tekla. Her mother, having found some strips of rubber in the stables, set about resoling everyone's shoes. She sat surrounded by jars of resin and cups of coffee and snake-like rubber peelings, and very soon everyone was hobbling round the house, forever tripping over their brand-new rubber soles.

Helena had a room on the ground floor – a dark, panelled room that looked out on to the park. There, she said, she spent her afternoons studying, elbows propped up on one of several volumes of European History in Polish, or Macaulay's *History of England*, or Bongand's *Le Christianisme et les Temps Presents*. She read steadily and well; and the books, the room and those uncertain months remained with her always, knotted together as a perpetual reminder of European turbulence.

Helena's mother had rediscovered an old friend from Wilno – Aunt Anna. Once, Aunt Anna had been very beautiful. Her emerald-green eyes and her long neck had always fascinated Helena and, as a girl, she had wished to be like her.

But now that Aunt Anna was nearly fifty, her face was bitter and her hair set in a wiry crown of marcel waves. When her husband had died, a few years earlier in St Petersburg, she had married a man ten years younger. Now she hated being seen with her children who reminded everyone how old she was. They were all in Wilno, her new husband was at the war and she and Helena's mother sat talking and smoking, playing cards and drinking endless cups of Turkish coffee.

In mid June Helena came in one lunchtime from the stable. A faint smell of apple blossom hung in the hall. Her mother was on the terrace with Aunt Anna, holding a letter.

'Your Dr Medeksa is in Wilno.'

'Let me see, Mama.'

The letter was written on thick, poor-quality paper and the ink had seeped a little into its fibres, fuzzing the letters. At the top were some lines in English from Keats. The letter ended:

> . . . I will remain in Wilno for another week, until
> 27 June. Come before then, Helena, I am waiting.
> Let me have your answer.
> Medeksa.

Aunt Anna waved her cigarette dismissively. 'Let her marry him! You have had enough trouble with her. Let her settle in some sordid flat in town while he treats Jews for venereal diseases!'

Helena took the letter away. She crossed the garden. She reached the shrubs and the wooden bridge beyond. She leaned against the parapet. She read the letter again and it left her cold. She could not marry him, not now. Everything was happening too fast; he was behind her.

Most of the time Aunt Anna wore evening frocks at Platków. She had no summer dresses. Her task was to restore the roses, and she wandered among them, smoking like a boatman, in a blue, puff-shouldered ball dress. Panna Konstancja, who had no time for Aunt Anna, said she looked like a redundant courtesan.

But no one had any clothes. All Helena's clothes had been lost. She had fled Minsk with nothing but her charcoal-grey mourning dress.

One day Freiherr von Sanden, the district commander, rode up to the house and presented her with a bale of sand-coloured linen – used for wrapping bread and cheeses. Panna Konstancja cut and pleated it into a skirt. She made a long loose blouse with a sailor's collar. In the village a shoemaker stitched a pair of linen boots, laced through a dozen eyes with hay-cord. The

German officers when they saw her, nicknamed her the '*Madel im Haafersack*'; Aunt Anna muttered about 'costumes for Warsaw bar-girls'.

Freiherr von Sanden came regularly to Platków that summer. He stood head and shoulders above any man Helena had ever seen; he must have been more than two metres tall. On his bay stallion, equally large, his Teutonic head brushed the chestnut boughs as he rode out of the avenue. When he arrived and greeted the women, his deep bow only brought his gaze down level with theirs.

In July, Freiherr von Sanden presented Helena with a fox cub named Lisek. He slept curled up in a rust-coloured ball on her bed. He behaved to her like a devoted dog. No one but Helena could get close to him. If anyone approached her room, he would leap out of the window.

But by October, Lisek had started to roam. He bullied the cats and chased the geese. At night he padded round the home-steads. When he began to kill hens and kittens Helena's mother said he must go.

Helena took him on a cart with Panna Konstancja and set him down deep in the forest; they shooed him away and he slunk off. Helena wept for him that night.

The next morning she opened her curtains, and there he was, panting at the window. She tried shutting him in the stables (he barked all night). She tied him on a long chain (he barked again). She made him a wire enclosure (he dug himself out).

For two days he hid beneath the verandah, in one of the ducts that ventilated the cellar. Helena let it be known that he had gone back to the wild, and smuggled him carrots and buckwheat from the kitchens. Then one of Ewa's geese was found dead.

'For goodness sake,' said Aunt Anna. 'Shoot the wretched animal!'

But Helena's mother took her side. They drove off again into the trees, into the *puszcza*. They drove for several hours and stopped by a small lake. The water was blue-grey and all around it was the green band of the forest. Her mother sat in the cart, while Helena took Lisek and set him down by the water. He lapped at it, looked up, then ran off into the trees without a backward glance.

Rumours of cruelty filtered up from the village. During the first year of occupation, the Germans had shot four men in the square for pilfering stores. Eva said the thieves had been Wehrmacht soldiers and that the villagers were innocent. Others, unable to bear the ignominy of occupation, had gone to live in the forest and sometimes they launched attacks on supply convoys. A number of houses had been burnt in retribution.

Then there was the story of Maria. Helena remembered Maria as a bright, rosy-cheeked girl with dark gypsy hair, always eating apples. She had been a kitchen maid at Platków. In the summer of 1916, she took to going down to the Wodalka lake where German soldiers met in the long evenings. Ewa had her beaten once; she warned her not to go. Maria continued to go, and then one day her body was found in some reeds. She had been strangled with her own hair-tie.

But for Helena, all this was hard to reconcile with the figure of Freiherr von Sanden. With him the war seemed far away. Sometimes he arrived, late on a summer afternoon, leading another saddle horse and they went out riding, over the low hills beyond the lake, across the fields and into the *puszcza*. He sang in a bass voice which boomed out among the trees. He sang for his schloss in the Rhineland and the black birds which spun around its towers.

All through August and September, once a week, Freiherr von Sanden took Helena riding. One evening, she remembers, they were coming back along the river. They dismounted, watered the horses and sat on the bank. He said, 'Winter is coming, Helena. Soon we must leave.' Then he turned to her and whispered, 'Come back to my castle on the Rhine with the black birds and the mist. Marry me, Helena.'

She was too surprised to answer.

'What do you say, Helena?'

She said no, she could not marry him. She did not love him. She was fond of him but she did not love him. She knew what love was now, real love, as for several weeks she had been in love with a man named Józef.

At that time, Józef was a man of about thirty-five. Part Lithuanian and part Tartar, he had a shallow v-shaped brow and dark skin. He had two estates, either side of Platków, and spent his time travelling between them in a green-painted *bryczka*. Whenever he passed Platków, he called in.

All that remained of a long line of hybrid nobility was Józef, and his mother who lived in Wilno. According to Helena, she was known as 'the best-dressed woman of Kresy' – despite having not risen from her bed since the day her husband died, fifteen years earlier.

Józef had inherited her elegance. Having no family at home, he would, when he was bored, pull on a nankeen frock coat and leap into his *bryczka*. He would go 'touring', an expression he used for turning up unannounced at any one of the neighbouring estates. Being unmarried and a great raconteur, he was usually welcome. But now that most of the *dwory* were abandoned, his 'touring' was confined to Platków.

In late August there was a spell of very hot weather. Between the heated-up days were heated-up nights. In the evening the Platków household gathered in a short-tempered silence on the verandah. On the second of these evenings, in the heavy light of dusk, Józef's *bryczka* had come rattling out of the avenue.

'Full moon and a warm night!' he cried, climbing the steps to the terrace. 'You know what that means?'

'Love . . .' sighed Aunt Anna.

'Crayfish!'

Józef asked Tekla to pack up some potatoes and, with three buckets, he led everyone down to the Wodalka lake.

The moon was fat and motionless on the horizon. Reeds stood thin-legged on the fringes of the lake. Among them, among these frail stalks, countless frogs conducted their languid debates.

The fire flared quickly. It sent sparks up out of the birch logs to glow briefly against the stars. Tekla cut some stakes for a sway and hung two kettles of water over the flames. Aunt Anna sat beside it with Helena's mother, a flask of black coffee, and two packets of Turkish cigarettes.

Józef took Helena and her sister to the lakeside and, instructing them to jump up and down on the banks, lay flat on the ground with his bare arms trailing in the water. The crayfish wriggled away from the bank and he snatched them out.

Józef was a brilliant mimic and later, in the firelight, while they cracked open the warm shells, he resurrected Wilno society with such skill that it seemed as if the war had never happened. The night echoed with Aunt Anna's laughter.

It was after midnight when Józef found Helena alone by the lake. He took her hand. 'Hela, I love you. I love your silky hair and your thin arms and the freckles on your nose. I love your distant look and the stars in your eyes. I love you, I love you, I love you.'

And that was that. The next day he left. Helena was baffled. Whenever he came again to Platków, the same thing would happen: he would behave as normal towards her until they happened to be alone. Then he would take her hands and tell her of the agony of his heart and the depth of his love. But not once did he ask her to marry him.

It took Stefan, the coachman, to notice what was happening. 'That Count Józef comes here too often. What's to come of it, Panna Helena?'

'I don't know, Stefan.'

'No good, I tell you. He should spend more time fixing his leaking roofs than here, troubling you.'

'But supposing I married him, Stefan? You could come and work for us and divide your time between here and there!'

'Marry him? That old Tartar bankrupt? May he be kicked by ducks! He has debts he will never escape.'

So that's it, thought Helena. That's why he has not yet asked me to marry him – his debts! And for this noble sacrifice, which inspired in her an admiration that was as profound as it was blind, she began to love Józef all the more.

15

THE SUMMER OF 1918 had been hot. The war was at a standstill and the country caught its breath. Helena watched the process of regeneration begin.

Each morning she walked down through the avenue, into the cherry orchards, across the fields to Mass. To begin with the fields were spread with rye- and barley-shoots. The shoots grew level with Helena's ankles, then her calves and her knees. In July the stalks dried and yellowed; the *parobcy* took down their scythes and in mid August swept across the fields in a slow twisting dance. They sheaved the crop and stood it in shocks while the sun dried it. Lines of rack wagons took the sheaves to the barns. In September everyone gathered in church to thank God for the harvest. They were all very nervous about the winter.

Throughout the autumn months, Touring Józef continued to profess his love for Helena. She felt content with him. His pressing attentions reassured her. She knew that as soon as his estates were back in order after the war, as soon as he was ready, he would ask her to marry him.

Poland became free. No one had dared predict what happened in Warsaw that November. On 11 November, the German occupation of Poland ended. The soldiers of the Wehrmacht were disarmed on the Warsaw streets. Piłsudski was released from prison, came to Warsaw and three days later was appointed Chief-of-State. For the first time since the eighteenth century, Poland was a sovereign state.

The news reached Platków on a frosty morning, with the

sound of hooves in the chestnut avenue. Freiherr von Sanden came out of the trees on his bay stallion. He swung down from the saddle. He stepped up to each of those gathered on the steps. He kissed the hands of the women, shook the hands of the men. Then he bowed to them all and remounted. His stallion shuffled back, tried to rear, and von Sanden cried, 'May God bless Poland! God bless you all!'

And he swivelled his horse around and left, riding out of the avenue, out of their lives, back to his black birds and his misty schloss on the Rhine.

In December, Uncle the Bishop arrived at Platków from Warsaw. He had been appointed Bishop of Riga and, while he waited to take up his new see, was accompanied by a young chaplain whose task it was to teach him Latvian. The chaplain was pale and thin and very shy. In the evenings, when Uncle Augustus sat playing chess with Helena, she would watch the chaplain shuffling round the edge of the drawing room, stalking his bishop with a textbook of Latvian grammar.

At Christmas, Mass was said in Platków's large hall. Uncle the Bishop stood on the stairs. The chaplain was on the step beneath, clutching the chalice. Three soldiers – two amputees and an artillery-deafened subaltern – sat at the foot of the stairs, while others crowded the hall and the corridors beyond.

Villagers lined up afterwards to kiss his amethyst ring. Unsure of how to treat a bishop they left him honey and eggs, which he accepted with delight, before directing these gifts back to the village through different channels.

The day after Christmas, Uncle the Bishop left Platków to go to Wilno for his investiture. Helena and her mother went with him, the three of them driven by Stefan in the old *bryczka*.

Years later, Helena concluded that this was the coldest journey she ever took. Each day the wind blew hard from the north-east. The muzzles of the horses froze and turned white.

Stefan's beard filled with icicles. Huddled in the open carriage in thick furs, Helena watched the ceaseless parade of frosted branches, the grey skies, the frozen lakes. The whole thing took three days.

The first night they spent in an inn run by an elderly Jewish couple. Because of the cold, everyone gathered in one room. They ate stuffed pike and drank Jewish mead. The windows were patterned with hoarfrost. After they'd eaten, the old man scraped at a fiddle and sang. Then they laid out their furs, and with the wolves baying from the forest, settled down to sleep.

That night Helena dreamt of her father. He was trying to tell her something; he was standing on the edge of a frosty wood and shouting, but his words were lost in the wind. She struggled to get closer but the snow was too thick. She dragged her legs; she twisted and lurched. The snow would not release her. Her father stood unmoving on the trees' edge, calling. She woke and pulled the fur up to her chin. She lay there for a while, watching the embers of the fire. In the morning one of the horses was found frozen to death in its stall.

They arrived in Wilno exhausted. Everything had changed. Their own house on Mała Pohulanka was shuttered up and deserted. They took a couple of rooms in the home of Madame Jelenska, known as 'the Pope of Wilno' on account of her passion for good works.

Wilno itself was neglected and grey. The colours of its buildings had faded; rust stains ran down the walls. Those few people who shambled through the uncleared snow were dressed in ragged shawls and scarves. Hollow-cheeked soldiers of the Lithuanian army patrolled the streets, surprised as anyone to be wearing the uniform of their own country.

'These Lithuanians,' scoffed Helena's mother, 'they have no idea how to be gay. If they were Poles, they would know how to celebrate!'

Uncle Augustus's investiture took place the following day.

The cathedral of Sw Stanisław was icy cold, but full of people. Helena borrowed a long grey skirt and a dark felt toque. She wore an aquamarine necklace. She stood with her mother close to the front. She watched Uncle Augustus prostrate himself on the steps of the altar, his chin in the dust. She watched the priests hover over him with candles. She heard the strains of the choirs, the thunder of the organ, and felt the old glow of her pre-war piety.

After three hours Uncle Augustus, now Bishop of Riga, turned to face the congregation. He raised his arms to give the blessing. A whisper rustled in from the back of the cathedral. It ran down the side aisles, in amongst the green and white columns. It spread into the domed chapel of Sw Kazimierz with its blood-red marble walls, its silver statues of Polish kings.

'Riga has fallen! The Bolsheviks have taken Riga!'

So instead of taking up his new see, Uncle Augustus went back with the others to Platków. He loaded his cope, his casket of pectoral crosses and rings, and hauled himself up onto the *bryczka*. They then drove another three days through the snow-crusted forests.

The following days at Platków – the last few days of Christmas – were a whirl of activity. Everyone was dusting down their high spirits; they hid the years of destruction; briefly, they forgot about the Bolsheviks. There were dancing parties and parlour games, and in the afternoons they pulled toboggans across the park to the small hills. They skated on the lake. At meal-times people stood and gave tear-sodden accounts of the refugee years, of staggering odysseys and chance encounters, of the dizzying shock of return.

One evening Touring Józef came and spun Helena around the ballroom in a wild écossaise. He professed his undiminished love and gave her a spindly-legged fawn.

The fawn delighted Helena – more so for a time than Józef

himself. She called him Pierre – she was reading *War and Peace*. Later Pierre turned out to be a girl, so he became Natasha. Helena kept Natasha in an unused stable on the edge of the woods and each morning waded through the snow to feed her.

The first threat to this new-found harmony came on the sixth day after Christmas. Helena's mother ran out of cigarettes. Like everything else that couldn't be grown, tobacco was still unavailable. Helena's mother had been living off a box of Italian cigarettes Uncle Augustus had acquired from a visiting monsignor. The whole household watched anxiously as she smoked the last ones. It was Uncle Augustus who saved the day. He discovered some mysterious herb with a strong flavour and rolled her cigarettes from this.

'Augustus,' she said, 'I don't know what this is, but it is wonderfully aromatic. You must tell me your secret!'

'Bishop's oath,' he said, and tapped the side of his nose.

But a week later she found out. He had been taking the hay from Natasha's litter. After that whenever Uncle Augustus tried to speak, she would say:

'Oh, shut up, Augustus! Remember that the Holy Ghost only speaks through you in your diocese.'

But there were deeper threats to which Helena said she was largely indifferent. She was much too involved with her deer. In early February, at a party given for her own name-day, Helena's mother stepped into the drawing room. She stood by the piano and called for silence.

'The Bolsheviks', she announced, 'are within two days' march.'

Everyone, remembers Helena, adopted their most serious expressions. Aunt Anna cocked her chin and straightened her back. Uncle Augustus led a short series of prayers. The women tried hard to look brave to each other; the men tried even harder, promising the greatest sacrifices for wives and families that they usually ignored.

Old Pan Romauld, with his squeaky voice, became particularly gallant. 'I will fight to the last to defend my land! I will not let this Godless mob violate my people!'

Helena and her sister nudged each other and giggled.

Uncle Augustus, seeing them, muttered, 'Youth fears nothing as it understands nothing!'

But for a time everything was quiet. Several weeks later, Helena developed a high temperature. That winter's 'flu epidemic reached her before the Bolsheviks. Her mother blamed it on 'her damned deer' and with Helena in bed, released Natasha into the forest.

Uncle Augustus worked out a plan with Stefan. If the Russians arrived, they would take the back drive to the village, and there hide as peasants.

But the Bolsheviks, when they came, came swiftly. There was no time to escape. A small unit of Red Army troops rode up out of the avenue one dusk. Helena was too ill to be moved.

Uncle Augustus never left her bedside. Downstairs Stefan and Ewa kept the soldiers at bay. They took over the dining room, ate most of the food in the house and, thinking it some expensive Polish liqueur, drank the shoe resin of Helena's mother.

In the middle of the night, the O'Breifnes fled Platków. They harnessed a farm cart and headed west. Helena remembers sitting propped against the side of the cart and the rain and the bare fields. She remembers the sound of the wheels in the mud and the figure of Uncle the Bishop, silent and stony-faced in the dawn light.

It was mid morning by the time they reached the German positions. Two days later they were on a train bound for Warsaw.

THE O'BREIFNES SPENT the spring of 1919 in Warsaw, free Warsaw. Warsaw was alive that spring. The squares were full of debates, the newspapers full of rhetoric; the banks of the Vistula were spotted with dandelion. Helena spent much of her time studying, her sights set on Cracow University.

Meanwhile, all the strain of the past months fell from her mother. She discovered a new brand of Polish cigarettes and became suddenly happy and benevolent. She bought Helena a white cotton dress and a white hat and took her to a Jewish photographer near the old palace.

In Cornwall, Zofia still has this photograph; it is the one where Helena is toying with her necklace. Her head is tilted slightly to one side; she looks coy and vulnerable. But in her eyes is a cool determination. There is something about the photograph, something about her, which makes you want to look at it again and again, and no one looked at it more than Helena herself; she admitted that it puffed her vanity to such a degree that if she passed a group of soldiers without turning their heads, she became quite petulant.

At about this time, Piłsudski left Warsaw and went east. He planned to take Wilno. Through a series of cunning manoeuvres and cavalry assaults, he sent the Bolshevik garrisons into confusion. After two days of street fighting, the Red Army withdrew. Piłsudski – himself from Wilno – issued a proclamation:

> I, who was born in this unhappy land, am well
> acquainted . . . with its state of perpetual subjection
> . . . Now at last in this land which God seemed to
> have forsaken, liberty must reign . . . The Polish Army
> brings Liberty and Freedom to you all . . .

Not everyone agreed. The Lithuanians saw the Poles not as liberators but occupiers. The eastern borders of the new Polish state, swelling though they were, were far from secure. Helena's mother was in no hurry to return. In May she took the family south for the summer, to a cousin's estate near Cracow.

The house, said Helena, was like Platków before the war: intact, with glass-fronted walnut cabinets, Chinese painted screens and gleaming silver. She hated it. It only served to remind her that they still had no home, that their own land was being fought over, that they had no money.

Added to that, Aunt Wanda, who owned the house would say things like, 'Of course, Helena's looks are the kind that don't last,' or, 'Intelligence is all very well in a man, but in a woman it merely brings bad luck.'

Helena wrote to the Ursuline convent in Cracow. She said she'd taught English in St Petersburg and Mother Augusta agreed to take her on. She travelled down on the train and was given a small, blue-wallpapered room with a bed and a desk. She loved that room. Her new independence brought out in her a passion for neatness, and she stacked her books according to size, aligned her three pairs of shoes like soldiers on parade, and started a diary. On the opening page she wrote, in English: 'The Story of Helena O'Breifne, teacher of English, lover of animals, residant [sic] of the House of Ursuline Nuns, ancient city of Cracow, Poland.'

And on the next page:

How the Dear Good Helenka spends her day!

7am. Mass.
7.30. Breakfast with the nuns (Milk, bread,
       cherry jam).
8am–noon. Teaching at convent.
12.30. Lunch (in a dairy – soup, pasta,
       dumplings).
2pm–4pm. University (History with Professor
       Rydel).
4.3pm–10pm. Private pupils.
10.30pm. Cold supper at convent (*kielbasa*,
       cheese), prepare lessons.

She kept an account of her earnings and expenditure in a
little red notebook, and each month took half of the difference
and put it in the *Dla Biednych*, the convent's poor fund. The
rest she saved and by November had enough to award herself
a dove-grey dress, kid gloves and two pairs of shoes. She carried
on a weekly correspondence with Józef, had her hair cut fashion-
ably short and never let go of the idea of university. Professor
Rydel was confident she could start the following year.

At the end of the school term, Helena took the Red Cross train
up to Wilno for Christmas. Reassured by the Polish adminis-
tration, her mother had returned there in October, with her
brother, sister and Panna Konstancja. Their own house on Mała
Pohulanka was still closed up. They lodged again with Madame
Jelenska, the Pope of Wilno, and Helena was given a room
overlooking an abandoned garden. A lime tree scratched at the
outer window with its branches. Inside the window Helena set
up a desk, and made two piles of books, one of English history,
the other of French.

There was to be a ball that Christmas, a charity ball. Helena's
Aunt Marynia was head of the Red Cross and, in the second
week of December, she kept them all occupied making red and

white paper-chains. She named the ball simply 'Ach!' and asked Helena to tell fortunes.

For this she wore Cracow national costume – a black velvet waistcoat and a white shirt, a red floral skirt and black lace-up boots. With eye shadow and cerise lipstick, she hardly recognized herself. She practised a Carpathian accent and learnt a repertoire of Romany expressions.

The night of the ball was 18 December. Thick snow fell for the first time that winter. It blew noiselessly against the winter windows. The streets were soft and silent. There were no sledges and no carriages; the war had taken all the horses. In the portico of Aunt Marynia's home, a great puddle spread out around the rows of felt boots.

Across the ceiling of the ballroom were strung the red and white paper-chains, arranged in a cross. It was very cold to begin with, and you could see people's breath as they talked. Nurses stood at one end behind the chairs of crippled soldiers. Aunt Marynia, wearing a red-crossed bib over her ball gown, stood on a bench and clapped her hands for silence.

'Ach!' she said, and a murmuring laugh swelled up from the room. 'You may wonder why this evening has been named "Ach!" Perhaps you think it is because I could think of no other name. Or that it is a reminder, after all these years of uncertainty, that we have lost our capacity for surprise. Well yes, those are reasons. But really it was just that whenever I mentioned the ball to people, they were lost for words. They looked at me as if I were mad and said, "Ach!"

'So with God's blessing, enjoy yourselves! Soda is served in the hall and there will be a prize draw at ten o'clock – first prize, a Jack-in-the-box from Vienna!'

The murmuring rose again and a quartet started to play. A line formed at Helena's table. One of the first in it was Touring Józef.

'So, gypsy girl, tell me my fate!'

She laid out his cards and looked at them a long time. 'You have led a lucky life. You have had many joys, and known many fine people.'

'You speak only the truth, gypsy!'

'But here, I see your heart is tired of wandering . . .'

He laughed. 'Oh, you have the wisdom of Solomon!'

'And this card, the nine of spades – you know what that means?'

Touring Józef threw up his hands in mock bewilderment.

'A big decision – something to choose, something to lose.'

Józef laughed, squeezed her hand, and disappeared back into the throng.

A little later another familiar figure stepped up to Helena's table. It was Adam Broński.

Four years had passed since Helena had last seen Adam, since the first morning of the flight into Russia. He was now thirty. His sisters had kept her up to date with his news, of his brave endeavours with the resistance during the war, of a riding accident, and his unhappy love for a certain Miss Gigant. This woman, red-haired and 'famously beautiful', was the daughter of the owners of Minsk's only cinema. In the autumn of 1917, Adam had fallen in love with her. There was talk of marriage, but that winter she had developed tuberculosis. Adam had sat by her bed every day for weeks. He had watched her die. Since then, said his sisters, he spent his days sitting in darkened rooms, playing his guitar.

As he sat down at Helena's table, Adam gave her a faint smile; he did not recognize her.

She laid out his cards. 'Well, I see a riderless horse . . . and here, two queens beside each other . . . you have lost a great love . . . I see a building, perhaps a theatre, and here, death waiting in the wings . . .'

And she carried on, mapping out the details of Adam's recent history, while he, still not recognizing her, listened incredulously to every word.

Józef came up, and put his hand on Adam's shoulder. 'So, my friend, will you marry a princess or die on the battlefield?'

'It is uncanny, Józef – how much she sees!'

Józef laughed. 'Adam, are you blind? You do not know who this is? It is Helena O'Breifne!'

When he looked at her again, it was with a strange mixture of surprise and respect. And, according to Helena, he kept that look for her until the very day he died.

Christmas of 1919 was like a homecoming. Helena felt for the first time in years that she belonged. Wilno was full of familiar faces. There were parties and dances, and skating in the Bernardyński Park. Everyone exchanged stories of the war.

The most disturbing story, or at least the one that remained sharpest in Helena's mind, came from Witek, a distant cousin.

Witek's family had bred horses before the war. When the Bolsheviks arrived last year they had taken the horses out into the stable yard. One horse, an Arab stallion, had suddenly enraged the Bolshevik commander. He stormed across the yard. He picked up a scythe, said Witek, and with four strokes, sliced through the stallion's neck.

'Why?' Helena asked. 'I mean, how can a horse cause such anger?'

'Because', said Witek, 'he was too beautiful.'

Before long, Witek had become a frequent visitor to the Pope of Wilno's house. Helena's mother noticed long before Helena. 'So, Hela, another corpse! They fall like pigeons at your feet. You really should be more careful.'

Later, Uncle the Bishop took her aside and, half in jest, said, 'Three of them – Józef, Adam and Witek. Which one will you marry?'

'None!' said Helena. 'I'm going back to Cracow to study for university!'

And that, she honestly believed, was what would happen.

But in February, she went down with a heavy cold and had to
delay her return; by March the cold had become pneumonia.
She lay in bed for two weeks while the lime branches tapped
at the window. When the doctor came, he said that tuberculosis
had developed in one lung.

She could not return to Cracow. Her mother telegrammed
the nuns and told them, with some satisfaction, that they would
have to find a replacement. Helena lay there for days. She gazed
at the lime branches. She gazed at the clouds. She thought, 'I
cannot live any more like this, I cannot live forever under her
wing.' And in her weakened state, dismissing her options one
by one, she decided: 'I must get married.'

These were the circumstances, according to her own account,
of Helena's engagement.

It was a clear spring day. She lay in bed. Her room was full
of sunlight. She wrote a note to Touring Józef urging him to
come at once. Panna Konstancja took the note across Wilno
and within an hour Józef was at her bedside. He brought flowers
and laid them on her bed. She told him immediately what she
wanted.

'Dear Helenka,' he said. 'I cannot marry you. My love is
too great to cause you such suffering. I am old and full of
debts. I would make a useless husband. You must marry
Adam.'

But when he had left she wrote to Witek. Panna Konstancja
went off again. This time she came back alone: Witek had left
that morning for the front.

So she wrote to Adam; he entered her room with a wide and
impulsive smile.

She said to him, 'Adam, you must listen carefully to what I
have to say. I would like us to be married. I will make you a
good and dutiful wife. I will look after you and serve you and,
God willing, give you a family. I will devote my life to that

family. But I do not love you. I need to marry to escape the trap of my mother.'

The two of them looked at each other and for a moment there was silence. Then Adam took her hand, and said, 'Hela! Don't worry, my love is enough for two!'

And so they were engaged. Helena's mother was delighted. She sent word at once to old Pan Broński, who arrived the following day. He went up to Helena's room to congratulate her. 'Splendid! I'll send you a horse for a son, a goat for a daughter!'

Two weeks later she was still in bed. It was a breathless day. A maid was taking off the winter windows. Helena could hear the birds outside and the maid saying, 'Birds are divided into crows and rooks. Those down there are rooks, Panna Hela, see. You can tell from their beaks, is what my mother told me . . .'

The door opened. It was Witek. He was wearing his uniform. He dismissed the maid and, grinning broadly, sat on Helena's bed.

She shook her head; she told him she was engaged. Unclipping the medallion of Our Lady from her neck, she pressed it into his hand. 'May God protect you, dear Witek.' And she turned away to weep.

17

HELENA SPENT the spring at Platków: 'April 1920. Violets
everywhere. In the avenues hens and chicks, and duck in the
Wodalka lake. Each day the green haze of the forest thickens;
the birch trees are coming into leaf . . .'

She and Adam had a turbulent engagement. Sometimes she
hated him – and told him so – for his perpetual high spirits,
for frustrating her plans to go to Cracow to study, for not being
any of the men she had loved. She wrote to him once breaking
off the engagement, and he had come from Wilno immediately,
riding out of the avenue and up to the house with a smile
stretched across his ever-trusting face.

'Burzyczka! My stormy storm-petrel! You have nothing to
fear!'

In mid April Adam left Wilno to go south. He had been
appointed a judge in Lida. His father had also made over a
house and land to him and, whenever he could, he went over to
prepare it for Helena's arrival. The estate was called Mantuski.

Helena knew Mantuski; she had stayed there in 1912. She
remembered the house and its long, low front, its dark old-
fashioned rooms; she remembered the corridors smelling of old
meat. It wasn't somewhere she'd warmed to at all. The only
good thing she could think about it was its position on the
banks of the Niemen.

The estate, said Adam, derived its income from a fairly even
split between its timber and its dairy herd. The cheeses – 'like
great cushions' – had been famous in Kresy before the war. But
it wasn't very profitable; there was not enough land. Of the

three Bronski estates it was the smallest. Adam's father had considered him 'too free with money' to trust him with the larger ones. That Adam – the eldest – should be by-passed like this infuriated Helena. But Adam, as always, didn't appear to mind.

He wrote to Helena:

> 20 April. Mantuski.
> Helenka my dearest,
> I am buying tiles for the house. The old tile factory was ruined in the war. New cows are coming from Gdańsk. The floods have come and tomorrow we start to plough . . . How I wish you could be here to see it. Oh Hela, Hela, Panna Hela! The world has never been so marvellous for me! It is ten days until we meet! I think of your hair and its little curls on your neck and your eyes. Aj! One look from them kills all my sadness. I kiss your hand, your two hands. I long to be with you. Do not fear, my little bird, my darling Helenka.
>
> Yours forever,
> Adam

*

The wedding was set for July. Helena's mother became very excited about the plans. Aunt Anna was back at Platków and the two of them sat hunched over the card-table, playing dominoes and discussing the guests, while the cigarette smoke hung over their heads like a rain-cloud.

Aunt Anna was full of stories for Helena. 'At eighteen, you know, boys are sent to women by their fathers. You'll soon find out what Turkish habits they picked up.'

Panna Konstancja was gathering what she could for Helena's

trousseau, stitching cotton tea-dresses and handkerchiefs and raiding the attic for bed linen.

In June Adam came to stay for two weeks before the wedding. With him was his cousin Józef Kossak.

They brought worrying news. The Red Army was massing again in the east. Budyonny had already attacked the Polish forces to the south, in the Ukraine. But it was in Belorussia that the main thrust was expected. On 2 July, Tukhachevsky, Commander-in-Chief of the Russian forces, issued his orders:

> Soldiers of the Red Army!
> The time of reckoning has come.
> The army of the Red Banner and the army of the predatory White Eagle face each other in mortal combat.
> Over the dead body of White Poland shines the road to world-wide conflagration.

The attack on Poland was the Bolsheviks' first foreign adventure. The plan was to link up with the burgeoning communist cells in Germany, and thence into Western Europe. Only Poland stood in the way, a country that had only existed for the last two years, and one that had, by common consent, already grown well beyond its capacity to defend itself.

On 4 July, the Red Army crossed the Berezina and took Minsk. On the 14 July, the day of Adam and Helena's wedding, they swept into Wilno and the city fell. Not one of Adam's family was able to reach Platków. The chapel was practically empty.

Helena wore a simple white dress and a tiara made from lilies of the valley. Sparrows sang in the chapel's rafters; a blind fiddler accompanied the 'Ave Maria'. Helena walked up the aisle – just as the gypsy had predicted five years before – on the arm of Józef Kossak.

Uncle the Bishop performed the ceremony. He stood before

them, offering his blessing. 'Do not expect happiness, my children!' and his eyes filled with tears.

'Pathetic priest,' muttered Aunt Anna.

At the back of the chapel, sitting alone, with the face of someone who had eaten poison, was Touring Józef. A year later he was married to a war widow from Siena and went to live in Cannes. (Helena saw him only once, years later, in the late 1930s, a tired red-faced old man. She couldn't decide whether it was exile or the war widow that had destroyed him.)

Stefan had painted the Platków carriage. With all suitable horses taken by the cavalry, he had harnessed Siwka and Gniadka, Platków's surviving plough-horses.

At nine o'clock that night Adam and Helena stood on the Platków verandah. The dusk gave way to night and they stepped inside. Helena went up to bed in her usual room. Adam was given the room next door. Beyond him was Helena's mother, with Uncle the Bishop on the other side. Panna Konstancja was upstairs.

Adam entered Helena's room in a dressing-gown. He sat on her bed and kissed her. She kissed him and said politely, 'Goodnight, Adam.'

Then they knelt for prayers. He kissed her again on the forehead, and went back to his room.

Helena was still wandering the avenues with her rosary, gazing at the high trees, humming her breezy tunes, bending in the grass to pick flowers. It took Adam some time to explain, to gain her trust. She found the whole thing faintly comic. Their real honeymoon took place that winter, on a snowy night in a Warsaw hotel; and during the months in between, to Helena's great surprise, they forged a remarkable friendship, a friendship without secrets or conceits, whose boundaries grew with each day, and which provided the basis for the only real love she ever knew.

*   *   *

The day after the wedding it was hot again. Helena and Adam sat by the lake. Adam read out passages from Majewski's *Kapital*, and sang the 'Dubinoczka'. They talked about the future. At midday they walked back to the house. Five Lithuanian soldiers stood on the steps; they had come to intern Adam.

There was nothing anyone could do. They took him away and Helena saw the cart sliding off into the avenue, flickering between the chestnuts like a running trout.

'Damn those Lithuanians!' Helena's mother threw her cigarette to the ground.

That afternoon she and Helena went to see the district commander, a man with tiny eyes who divided his hatred evenly between Poles and landowners. Helena could see he was enjoying their misfortune.

'Pani Hrabina,' he said with mock respect, 'you must understand. The old countries are gone. Six wars are being fought around your beloved Poland and when they are over, all Europe will be one. Please, be patient.'

Patience was not something Helena's mother found easy. For three days she smoked and paced the verandah, until Adam appeared one morning from the trees. He had escaped the internment camp by pretending to be a doctor.

That same night they all left Platków, just as the year before, fleeing on farm-carts. Adam was keen to join his regiment. They travelled west, crossed the border into East Prussia and reached Gdańsk on a small fishing-boat; Helena was horribly sick the whole way. Several days later they were in Warsaw, where Adam kissed Helena on the cheek, and went to find the 13th Uhlans.

Such was the first week of their married life.

The Red Army was closing on Warsaw: six armies, more than 100,000 men, were moving rapidly towards it. All attempts to slow them had failed. Poland's brief independence was being shattered. Yet in Helena's account there is nothing about the threat, nothing but a list of who she saw and where she stayed and the fact that Warsaw seemed 'rather hot'.

Lord D'Abernon, head of an Allied delegation, recorded the same apparent nonchalance in his Warsaw diary of the time:

> 26 July. I continue to marvel at the absence of panic, at the apparent absence indeed of any anxiety . . . all the best troops are being sent to Lvov, leaving Warsaw unprotected.
>
> 27 July. The Prime Minister, a peasant proprietor, has gone off today to get his harvest in. Nobody thinks this extraordinary.
>
> 2 August. The insouciance of these people here is beyond belief. One would imagine the country in no danger and the Bolsheviks a thousand miles away.
>
> 3 August. The population here has seen so many invasions that it has ceased to pay any attention to them.

Examining his options two nights later, Piłsudski realized the only hope of defence was to attack. The orders were issued: a large part of the Polish troops were to disengage, hurry south along the front, and cut off the Red Army from the rear. The plan was an absurd one. Yet it worked.

The Miracle on the Vistula, as it became known, was a decisive victory. Never again was the Soviet army defeated so emphatically. There followed a bloody Russian retreat. The Red Army slid into disarray. The lands of Kresy were trampled by starving, leaderless Cossacks and retributive Poles.

By October 1920, an armistice was called and Poland found itself with an eastern border more than 500 miles long. Lord D'Abernon, who had witnessed the Polish victory, gave its importance a hyperbolic assessment:

The Battle of Tours saved our ancestors from the Yoke
of the Koran; it is probable that the Battle of Warsaw
saved Central and parts of Western Europe from a more
subversive danger – the fanatical tyranny of the Soviet.

In fact it proved only a respite, a twenty-year respite in which
the landed families of Eastern Poland carried on living much
as before.

Adam was demobbed in November. He came back to Warsaw
and burst into the flat with his customary enthusiasm. He and
Helena planned to leave for Mantuski. Helena had no clothes
but summer clothes. One day in the street she met her Uncle
Nicholas O'Breifne. He gave her some money for a winter coat,
but the money went instead towards the price of a black-eyed
dachshund puppy. Helena called the dachshund Haust.

The following morning, she and Adam and Haust left Warsaw on one of the first trains to the re-established territories of
Eastern Poland. They spent two days sitting on sacks of grain
from America, while Helena clutched her dog for warmth.

In Lida they stayed with a Jewish family. When she heard
where they were going, the old woman clapped her hands in
horror. 'Alone in the forest! How can you live there now?'

In the morning they left early. They loaded their few belong-
ings on to an old dray with low sides and a high box. They
told the Jewish family their horses would be back in a few days.

Helena remembered the journey well. It was bitterly cold.
An icy fog had paralysed the land. Nothing moved in that dead
November; the road was no more than a series of frost-hardened
ruts, the scars of a dozen armies. And yet, she said, everything
seemed hopeful and new: new home, new Poland, new dachshund, new Adam.

They rode in silence. The reins rested lightly in Adam's
gloved hands. His moustache had thickened in the army. His

high forehead rose steeply before shelving back beneath the peak of his peasant *czapka*. 'How he loved that *czapka*!' thought Helena. And always his grey eyes, hooded at the corners, bright with an eternal uncomplicated joy.

All morning the forests dozed beneath the fog. There was no one else on the road. Around midday the trees thinned and they entered a plain. A milky sun seeped through the cloud; the unworked fields wore thick fringes of grass. The road dipped and rose through a number of low hills.

They came to a small river; the bridge had been destroyed and the two horses placed their feet tentatively on the frozen water, which gave way. They crossed the river with the ice just above their fetlocks, breaking it with each step. Adam stood on the box to shout them on, and soon they were bounding up the far bank.

Sitting down again, he began to talk about Mantuski. He spoke of his visit there last year and the damage that he'd found. The Russians had used the house as a field headquarters and much of the furniture was destroyed. He had managed to arrange repairs and redecoration and ordered new furniture. 'You will like what I've done!'

The day slid into afternoon. In the colourless twilight, they pulled off the main road and onto a soggy track which threaded its way between the trees and out again into the homesteads of Mantuski village. The houses were low and brown. Each one was penned in by a square of picket fencing. Leafless trees were scattered among the houses; narrow streams of smoke rose from the chimneys. Helena waited to see her new house.

A cold wind blew through the pines. Broken ice lay across the Niemen. The sky was black as they pulled through the village towards the house. There was no house. *Nie ma domu.* Only the chimney of the brick factory remained. Not one other building. The house had been burned to the ground.

*   *   *

Helena says nothing about her or Adam's response. She says only that it was dark by the time they crossed the Niemen, and that they drove on through the night to Druków.

One or two of Uncle Nicholas's retainers were at Druków – Rymszewicz (who had led the convoy in 1915), his wife, Janówa the cook. They greeted Adam and Helena with tears.

Adam left early the next morning. He had to return the horses to Lida. A week later he was back, stepping out of the forest, crossing the fresh snow in the park and climbing up to the house. Two hares hung from his shoulder. He had spent a night or two at Mantuski; most of the estate workers were still in hiding. The rebuilding, he told Helena, would start at once.

18

MANTUSKI TOOK exactly three years to rebuild. In the meantime Adam and Helena lived at Druków, in the old estate office of Uncle Nicholas O'Breifne, a building known as the '*oficyna*'.

The first winter was the worst any of them had known – worse even than those of the war. The accumulated effect of the occupations, the offensives, the invasions and retreats, the revolution, had sucked the land dry. There was nothing. No cows, no horses, no pigs, no chickens, no corn; no mail and no trains.

To begin with, Helena had some American tins, most of which were fed to Haust. After that it was just buckwheat. This was boiled into a watery porridge, *kasza*, the traditional buffer against famine. '*Kasza* is our hope' went a popular saying, and Adam never tired of repeating it at table, as a joke, as he handed a bowl of it to Rymszewicz's young daughter, Kasia.

But Adam was only rarely at Druków. Each Monday morning of that winter he walked through the snow to Mantuski. There he spent the week with a peasant family in a *chata*, and set about clearing the debris from the *dwór*.

There was no consensus as to quite what had happened to Mantuski. Adam gleaned various reports from the villagers. It seemed that towards the end of September 1920, after the Battle of the Niemen, a great number of Russian troops had retreated along the river's southern bank. Polish cavalry pursued and harried them. At Mantuski, where there was a ferry, the Russians had slowed to cross the river and some sort of battle took place. When it was over, the *dwór* was in flames. No one could tell him who was responsible – Poles or Russian or looting villagers.

For Helena, virtually alone at Druków, the weeks dragged. She missed Adam. Each Saturday evening he came back from Mantuski for a couple of nights, shaking the snow from his boots and laying his gun on the table. For her, those nights were the only times during that dark winter that she felt truly alive.

In February 1921 Helena started to give classes to the village children. She taught them reading and writing, and small gifts began to arrive for her: a lump of bacon, some gritty bread, corn someone had managed to hide, a beetroot. And on one day there was a note, written in almost incomprehensible Polish, begging her to visit a girl's grandmother.

The grandmother was a large shapeless woman and she was very ill. She lay on the stove-bed, in a small cabin in the forest. Her family, being Tartars, had fled east during the years of war and now there was only this one girl.

'Help her, please,' whispered the recumbent woman. 'I am nearly through.'

Helena did what she could. She sent them food when there was any. The Tartar woman lived on. Always she was the same when Helena went there, pale and listless on her heated stretcher, but alive.

At dusk on a foggy day in March, she was returning from the old woman's cabin. A soldier in a ragged uniform stepped out of the mist and fell into step beside her.

The soldier was Polish. He had been living in the forest since his unit had been routed in the last Russian advance. He'd heard there was peace, but he didn't believe it.

'God has left this country,' he said.

'God is still here if you know where to look.'

'Among the trees I see only ghosts. The men that have fallen.

Those are the ones I know. Ghosts.' He looked down at his bast shoes and shook his head. 'I have no one. No one but ghosts. Stop here with me.'

She said nothing.

'Stop here,' he repeated, and stood in front of her. She was forced to halt. He raised one blackened hand and reached for her shoulder.

The wind sighed in the trees overhead; it was getting dark. Helena looked him in the eye. 'I too am a ghost. And if you meddle with a ghost, you can never return to the land of the living.'

His hand fell back to his side.

Days later the story reached Helena of a deserter running out of the forest, wide-eyed and chattery with some story about a ghost, a strange and amorous ghost, who had tried to accost him.

Around this time Stefan arrived from Platków. He was leading two mares, Siwka and Gniadka, the same two horses that had driven Helena and Adam from their wedding. She hardly recognized them; they stood in the yard, and the cage-bars of their ribs poked out through tettered flanks. Stefan said they were due for the wolves, but he knew she'd find a use for them.

'Oj-oj-oj!' She clapped a hand to her chin. 'What skeletons!'

Sick though they were, Siwka and Gniadka were the only two horses at all in that dead country. Helena cleared the old straw and cobwebs from the Druków stables. Three times a day she scrubbed the horses with a tobacco solution; she dabbed the sores with boric acid. Her friend the Tartar woman produced some flax oil and this she rubbed on; someone else brought salt, so they were given salt. She changed their bedding, groomed them, fed them, talked with them, prayed for them – and slowly, very slowly, a little life re-entered their tired eyes.

In mid March the wind went round to the south; the patches

of snow in the park disappeared; one or two mild days slipped in between the frosts. The fields, ungrazed and unploughed, appeared oblivious to the change in the seasons.

Meanwhile Kresy began to twitch with life. A weekly train now ran to Wilno and every now and then someone would return from Nowogródek with a letter. Helena received one from her mother. It was dated 20 March, and had come from Wilno:

> . . . Aunt Anna here, dreadfully unhappy. Everyone maddened by shortages. We have recovered the house in Mała Pohulanka. Come to Wilno, dear, while Adam rebuilds Mantuski. Your room is still here. In a few years you'll be wrinkled like an old *baba* if you live out there . . .

Helena declined.

One Saturday in late April, Adam arrived after his week at Mantuski, striding out of the avenue with a newspaper, six days out of date. He called the household together – Pan Rymszewicz and his wife, and the families of some of Helena's pupils. Standing on the steps, in the low afternoon sun, Adam pushed up his cap.

'From the Sejm in Warsaw! "In the name of Almighty God!"' he read. '"We, the people of Poland, thanking Providence for freeing us from one and a half centuries of servitude, remembering with gratitude the bravery, endurance, and selfless struggles of past generations . . . we hereby proclaim and vote this Constitutional Statute in the Legislative Assembly of the Republic of Poland."'

A faltering cheer rose from that small group and the women bent to kiss one another. Pan Rymszewicz hurried into the house. He came out with vodka and a tray of rattling glasses.

'A toast,' cried Adam. 'To Piłsudski! To Poland!'

'Poland! The republic!'

But there were one or two there who were not Poles, who did not share his enthusiasm, and slipped away, muttering, to their bare-shelved homes in the village.

After that winter, Helena and Adam had the feeling, unstated though it was, that things could never be quite so bad again. In their private conversations, they spoke only of the future. The past was a shadowy place and neither of them wanted to revisit it.

In April Helena walked over to Mantuski with Adam. It was the week before Easter. The Niemen was high from the flood, and Gregory the ferryman had quite a battle getting them across the river.

At the site, there was little sign of progress. It had been cleared; there was a stack of charred timber by the trees; the old walls had been knocked down, and the *parobcy* had started to sort the stone. But they were short of everything – materials, tools and time. Helena was dismayed to think how long it would all take. She returned to Druków full of plans, and one of these was to establish an apiary.

A week or so later, Rymszewicz found a swarm in the bole of an old oak. They hacked out the section at night. They set it on wooden supports in the orchard and in the morning made a skep and three frames. Helena, waving a faggot of smoking reeds, stepped up to transfer the swarm to the skep. She cut out the wax with the eggs in it, carried it to the hive and placed it inside. Then she dropped the reeds and fled.

But the bees got in under her veil; she was badly stung. For three days afterwards, she could hardly see. Her temperature soared to 104°. After a week a doctor came from Nowogródek. Pani Rymszewicza showed him into the library where Helena lay on the sofa. He examined her, washed his hands, and said she would start to recover soon. He also announced that she was three months pregnant.

'Lord!' Pani Rymszewicza sat down hurriedly. 'And after all them bee stings! What manner of creature will you produce?'

'One used to suffering,' joked Helena.

But in truth she was terrified. She sent a message to Mantuski, and two mornings later Adam burst into her room having walked through the night. His hair was lank and, when he took off his *czapka*, tufts of it stuck out at strange angles. 'I want a dozen children!' he cried.

'No, Adam Broński! I am not a machine.' But she too was smiling.

Adam threw open his arms and yelped with joy.

To begin with, Helena was frequently sick. She lost weight, and her cheekbones tented out the pale skin of her face; she became very bad tempered.

In May the potatoes were dug at Druków; their muddy white bodies signalled the first real sign of life from the dead land. The lilacs came out beside the lake and Helena grew a little stronger; she walked whenever she could and trailed her hands through the high grass.

At the same time, life at Druków moved towards its old pre-war normality. Uncle Nicholas returned from Warsaw. Helenka the maid and the Angora cats Kiki and Risetka came by train from Wilno; the brother of Pan Rymszewicz, who had lost an arm in 1916 in the Russian trenches, returned. Rymszewicz himself travelled west to Poznan and returned after six weeks with twenty cows and three horses. Uncle Nicholas gave Adam one of the horses, and three cows for Mantuski. For the rest of the summer at Druków there was milk and butter and the first cheeses, and Helena's cheeks swelled again; she became breathless and clumsy.

Then, in September, Panna Konstancja, despatched by Helena's mother, arrived in a battered old *tachanka* with two ten-pound hams on the seat beside her.

It was agreed that the baby should be delivered in Wilno and in early October, with Adam and Haust, Helena travelled up there. They stayed in the house on Mała Pohulanka. With the first frost came Helena's contractions and Adam took her to the Doctor Rymsza hospital. All evening her labour continued. Adam was horrified by her pain. He could not bear to watch, so at dusk slipped off to the Church of Sw Yakub to pray. He prayed and prayed and prayed. Then he fell asleep. He woke to find himself locked in. All night he was stuck in that church and when at last he was released, at eight in the morning, he hurried to the hospital, fully expecting Helena to be dead.

But she was sitting up. She had had a ten-and-a-half-pound baby, a daughter. Adam knelt beside the bed and wept.

Adam's father and Helena's mother, their two remaining parents, were her godparents. She was christened in Wilno: Zofia Aleksandra.

At Druków when they returned, there was a carriage waiting for them in the yard. A face leaned out through the window, chewing on a carrot. It was the bearded face of a goat. The coachman handed Helena a letter, headed with the Broński crest:

'A goat for the birth of your daughter, Zofia Aleksandra. Stanisław Broński.'

PART III

MANTUSKI

19

IN EARLY JANUARY 1993, Zofia received a letter from a cousin of hers in Poland. Would she come and join her for a couple of weeks that summer, at a spa in Lithuania?

She telephoned me to ask what I thought. 'You know, Pheelip, what I'd really like to do? I'd like to see Wilno, where I was born. According to me, this spa is only about a hundred miles to the west. If I could get a bus or something . . .'

I had to be in Russia that summer. I told her I could come down and collect her and we could go together.

So on the eve of the longest day, a battered Soviet bus left me in the small Lithuanian spa town of Birstonas. I crossed the square and headed towards the river. The poplars were shaking their leaves in the wind; a rainstorm had just passed over the town and black puddles lay across the road.

Beyond the town was a complex of concrete hotels. I found the right one, took the lift to the fifth floor, walked down a darkened corridor and knocked on the door of Room 511.

'Pheelip! I thought you'd never make it!'

I kissed Zofia on both cheeks and followed her into the room. She was wearing a pale blue skirt and a navy sweater and a string of plastic beads. She turned and sat down. Her face, with its network of lines, the etched-out legacy of a lifetime of charm and suffering, was tanned and glowing. I said she looked well.

'Yes, I am. But I tell you, two weeks here and it is enough! It is stul-tifying here. If it wasn't for my books and the Niemen, I think I would have gone mad.'

On the table in front of her were two or three stacks of books. I could see the poems of Zbigniew Herbert, a new book by Kapuściński and a biography of Daphne du Maurier: Polish and English; Poland and Cornwall, her two worlds. I asked if she had been writing.

'Yes, a few verses. But only in Polish.'

That evening we spent with her cousin and a couple of other Polish widows. We sat in one of their rooms and drank a bottle of Dubonnet. We ate chocolate. The late sun came through the window and fell on the widows' grey hair and on their old-fashioned dresses; and the bottle went round the group and they told their stories, the fifty-year-old stories, the same stories that sooner or later every conversation turned to here – the stories of deportations and exile and death – until it seemed there was nothing more to say. Silence flooded between us. From the outside came the sound of a truck changing gear and Zofia smiled, saying: 'Come on, enough gloom! A song!'

She sang her Belorussian song, and then one of the women started the 'Red Belt' and gradually the others joined in. Their voices stretched across the evening, spilling out of the open window and down towards the river. They made a strange medley, those Polish widows, the one with a mannered soprano, another with a plaintive mumbling voice, another spirited and sharp. I thought of their stories as they sang and looked at their faces – at the one whose husband had died a month before, and the one whose mother-in-law had been crushed beneath a German tank, the one whose family had all died in Auschwitz, the one who'd been deported to Kazakhstan and saw a woman in the cattle truck slash her own throat.

The singing finished and I noticed in Zofia's eyes a familiar mist of tears. 'My God,' she said, 'just think how lucky we've all been! What a charmed life we've led!'

'Lucky?' I blurted. 'How can you say that, Zosia!'

She shook her head. 'No, Pheelip. Just consider. Why was it that we were spared while all those others perished?'

The next morning we left Birstonas and the Polish widows and took a bus up into a region of lakes and *kolkhoz* fields and forested horizons. Zofia was curious to see Vilnius. She called it by its Polish name, Wilno.

'It just shows you how stupid and unthinking I was as a girl. I never imagined Wilno was anything but Poland. We were never told in school how Piłsudski had just come and annexed it from Lithuania – and only the year before I was born!'

We topped a hill, and Vilnius was spread out before us – an archipelago of old church towers in a bay of new grey tower blocks.

We looked for the hospital where Zofia had been born but had no luck. Crossing the square in front of the old KGB headquarters, we reached the church of Sw Jakub. It was being restored. Inside, a network of wooden scaffolding rose up into the vaults like some elaborate stairway. A team of women was sweeping building-dust from the stone floor.

Zofia went up to them. 'Do you know,' she said, 'that seventy-two years ago, on the night I was born, my father came here – to this very church – and he prayed so hard that he was locked in all night! Imagine that!'

The women smiled at her, and looked at her clothes. They didn't understand a word of Polish.

'I wonder,' said Zofia, as we came out of the church. 'Mickiewicz street was somewhere here. We had a flat there – number sixty-two.'

I asked an ice-cream vendor what the street was called.

'Gedimino.'

'And before?'

'Before?' he scoffed. 'Stalin, Lenin, Hitler, you name it . . .'

'What about before the war? In Polish times.'

'Oh then! Then it was Mickiewicz.'

'So,' said Zofia, 'the block is down the other end. The last one before the river.'

It was a long way. Small blue plaques announced the numbers. We followed the evens down the left-hand side. Number sixty was opposite the new parliament building. But there was no sixty-two, just a wide-open space, the road and the river.

We stepped into the middle of the space. It was empty. Zofia looked around and shook her head.

'It's all so strange, Pheelip! You know, if I saw my sixteen-year-old self now, crossing this square, I really think she would be a complete stranger to me.'

We circled back along the river and into the old town. Zofia wanted to see the Miraculous Madonna. The chapel in which it hangs stretches over one of the old gates, 'The Gates of Dawn', the Ostra Brama. Outside were rows of beggars and a group of autistic children. A woman was struggling up the stairs on her knees.

Inside the chapel, Zofia stood for several minutes before the painting. The candle-light played on her face. All around her were the muttered devotions of the old, the ill, the curious, the trickling new recruits of post-Soviet Catholicism.

The image itself was extraordinary. As you looked at it – that tallow-faded face, encased in silver, with hooded eyes and tilted head (based, it is said, on the face of Barbara Radziwiłłóna) – it became sadder and sadder and sadder until it seemed as though no sadness could be too wide, no suffering too great for her to bear. The devotees and pilgrims, fingering the beads of their rosaries and mouthing incantations, stared at her as if in an inescapable trance.

Zofia stood apart from them, no rosary in her hands, no

incantations on her lips; on her face was an expression of loss that was so characteristic it was like a signature. I could never tell whether it was closer to tears, or laughter.

Beneath the painting, like a smile, was a silver crescent moon. All around it were panels and panels of gold and silver hearts, embossed names, praying figures, silver arms, legs, hands and feet – and messages: 'Thank you for listening to the prayers of my heart. St Petersburg 1912.'

That was the year Helena started to come here on her own. She was thirteen and had just begun to cross swords with her mother. At Ostra Brama, she wrote later, she could air her adolescent fury in an atmosphere of apparent understanding.

Outside it was raining, a soft rain which fuzzed the skyline and sat like dew on Zofia's grey hair. She put on a waterproof hat and tied it up under her chin.

'In the worst years of the war in London, Pheelip, I wrote a poem about the Madonna here. It won some prize or other. I can't think why, it wasn't all that good . . .' And she was smiling as we crossed the cobbles and went out through the gate.

One evening in Vilnius we met a Polish businessman and his wife. They were friends of friends in Warsaw. They had started a company importing processed food from France and Germany; it was going well. No, they said, there was no trouble for the Polish minority in Vilnius, not if you made good business.

We ate in a new restaurant. The waiters outnumbered the diners by at least two to one. We sat on chrome-and-leather chairs at a table of smoked glass. The businessman dabbed his mouth with a napkin, touched Zofia's arm and said, 'Afterwards we want to take you for a drive, we would like to show you the new buildings.'

It was dusk. We drove up out of the old town, past the avenue where Helena had lived in 1915, where she had watched the prize horses arrive; past the church where in 1918 she had prayed, piously, that all the chaos should end and had clutched her rosary so tight, she recalled, that it had left deep red marks in her palms.

'My mother lived somewhere here,' Zofia told the businessman. 'In 1915 and again in 1918.'

'Really?' he said.

'And I was born in a hospital somewhere there . . .'

'How interesting!'

But he didn't slow the car.

On towards the edge of town were the new buildings. The skyline was filled with them. They stood in ranks against the darkening sky, lights dim in the windows, their ordered façades defiant and cold, row upon row of them, like radiators waiting for installation.

The businessman's wife turned towards us. She was smiling. 'It is beautiful, yes?'

I nodded.

And then we were among them. Everywhere were cranes, stacks of pre-stressed concrete blocks, holes in the ground. The grey of the buildings fused with the grey of the sky. The buildings seemed interminable. We drove around one set of blocks and there was another, and another, until I imagined we were in some sort of grim modernist maze where the minotaur was a yellow earth-mover, Theseus a quantity surveyor, and his ball of string nothing more than a builder's extended tape measure.

'Just think,' said the businessman, grinning with the joy of it all, 'five years ago, this was just a village. A village! Now look!'

As if to illustrate his remark we reached the edge of the maze, suddenly, and the horizon dropped back to the forest. And there, lodged between the piles of torn-up turf, the concrete pipes, high and dry on an island of untouched ground, half hidden by fruit trees, was a wooden cabin. A dog was chained to the wall and in one of the windows a single light glowed through the curtains.

20

BY CHRISTMAS OF 1921, with the snow drifting against the banks of the Niemen, the rebuilding at Mantuski had to be abandoned. Adam returned to Druków. He took a post as judge in the village assembly. He continued it in the spring, leaving Bartek in charge of the work at Mantuski.

Adam and Helena spent two more winters in the *oficyna*. They were bright years, but austere. Poland at the time was pulling itself out of the mire of war and revolution and was settling into a more innocent routine of political squabbling. At Druków, no one was aware of much beyond the village.

Progress at Mantuski was made in fits and starts. The brick factory was working again, as were the timber yards. But sometimes the whole site lay idle for several weeks while they waited for cement, or a bucket, or a box of nails, or everyone left to plant or plough and attend to the more important business of trying to feed themselves.

Adam and Helena settled into the slow, convalescent rhythm of the land. Only one thing marred the process of regeneration and that was Helena's health. In the spring of 1922, she contracted pleurisy, and in the summer developed a haemorrhage in one lung. Trusting Zofia to Panna Konstancja and the goat's milk, Adam took Helena to a sanatorium in southern Poland. The doctors said she must stay six months.

Rabka sanatorium was an old *dwór* with high ceilings and long echoing corridors. Helena had a painting of Cracow above her bed and a sash window with broken shutters. The days were slow and heavy and Helena felt trapped – trapped by her own frailty, trapped by the distant mountains, trapped by the fresh-faced nurses. She longed for the forests and Druków and Mantuski; she longed for Adam and Zofia and the animals. She wrote letters:

19 May. Rabka sanatorium.
Adam darling,
It seems I've been here a hundred years, each day is exactly like the last. I go to my meals. I come back to my room. I read until my eyes ache from reading. I feel better, though in the afternoons I get so terribly tired . . .
Adam, I have let you down. What sort of mother am I to be, ill always and far from my child? Send me news, please. I think of you each moment and darling Zofia and Haust and everyone at Druków. Kiss them all for me!
Helena.

*

27 May. Druków.
Miraculous Helena! Your letter came today and I took it out and waved it in the wind. Don't be hard on yourself, *kochana*, don't look at yourself from the side . . . Imagine, this afternoon a shaggy-haired bandit was in the courtroom. He had tried to steal the priest's horse. While he was talking, and telling a tale about the priest's stables and his mother who had just died, I suddenly realized I was not listening at all but thinking of you! You were standing in your fur coat before the *oficyna* with your cheeks glowing against the snow. 'Helutka!' I muttered. 'Helutka!' The poor bandit thought I was quite mad! I had to

let him off . . . Haust has a very sad face and misses you very much . . .

*

1 June. Rabka sanatorium.

. . . Today I spent the afternoon on the terrace. The bees were tireless – what a din they made! I have been reading a lot. There is nothing else to do. Some of these Polish authors are really not worth it with their endless side-taking, but I adore the Scandinavians. I have been reading Ibsen. I have found a dear woman from Wilno who has some terrible wasting disease but we cheer each other with talk of Wilno and Mickiewicz. How are the horses?

*

11 June. Druków.

. . . I tried to harness Gniadka and she broke a swingle-tree, then she refused to plough, but Siwka went into harness like an angel. I sent eight hens to Mantuski today! The priest is very angry about the bandit, but how could I explain! Haust is fine. The baby is fine. But we all ask – where are you? Oh my love! My bird of passage! We all think of you. The world is wonderful when I am with you. What eyes I have, they see you everywhere! I will go now into the fields and look for your face in the buckwheat, in the pines, in the empty places of the forest. I kiss your lips, my darling. My lips are quite painful from kissing . . .

*

20 June. Rabka.

Adam darling, Everything is much as before. I look out of the window. I watch the clouds above the hills. What a torment it all is! I must leave this place. I think of Zofia's little white face and wonder why God has denied me her first months. A young soldier died here today, from a leg wound he received fighting the Bolsheviks. He looked about seventeen. There was a special Mass in the chapel . . .

*

1 July. Druków.
Darling Hela, I am in our room in the *oficyna*. It is the middle of the night. I have found a dressing-gown from before the war. The silence is buzzing in my ears. Zofia is asleep. Two days ago I went to Mantuski and the roof is almost finished! One hen died but the others are laying well. Tomorrow I must attend an autopsy. The doctors will cut up the corpse and I will ask questions. Ugh!
. . . Goodnight, my Hela, because the cocks are crowing. There are mice everywhere. We must buy mousetraps. I am very tired and my hand is slowing. Goodnight, my dearest love,
   Adam.

*

16 July. Rabka.
. . . I have decided to come home, Adam. The doctor will examine me again but he has said: 'I cannot force you to stay.' I take that to mean I can leave. I will let you know when I will return . . .

*

When Adam realized finally that she meant to come home, he travelled himself to the sanatorium. He wore a new coat and black polished shoes. He looked thinner. They sat for a long time on Helena's bed, talking too much and too quickly. Then they went in to see the doctor.

The doctor had half-moon glasses. He looked at them both, then peeled the glasses from his ears. He held out his hand to a pair of wicker chairs. 'Sit down, please . . . Pani Brońska, your lung is now healed. I would like you to stay another few weeks, but if you insist, well, what can I do?'

'Thank you, doctor.'

'But I must warn you that it would be very unwise for you to have any more children.'

Back at Druków, they consulted Uncle the Bishop. He consulted Rome. Months passed and Helena justified, in her own mind at least, that using birth control was all right; if it would save her, enable her to mother Zofia.

But the reply from Rome was unequivocal: 'The soldier dies on the battlefield, the woman in childbirth.' And within a few months, she was expecting another child.

That second winter in the *oficyna* was cold and dark and very long. Helena lay for days beneath her counterpane. She watched the black boughs of the beech tree brush against the sky. Half-completed cushion covers lay beside her. Zofia lay swaddled in a cot in the corner, Haust in his curled-up crescent before the fire; the wind prodded at the eaves.

Helena waited. She waited through the long mornings and the yellow dusks; she became indolent with waiting; in her darker moments she became convinced, alone in the wooden fastness of that cabin, that her whole life had been like this: a sentence, waiting for release.

In March, release was given. She gave birth, without any hint of complication, to a son; a week later, a three-year-old mare was standing in the Druków yard, the gift of Adam's father.

Helena's account of her early life ends at about this time. Pictures of the 1920s and early 1930s – the first ten years at

Mantuski – emerge from her papers of the time: letters, stories, scraps of diary, all the bits and pieces that survived the escape. Certain important events she chose to write up in detail, and one of these was the move to Mantuski. She had chosen for it the pages of a small green, leather-bound notebook. At Braganza, Zofia had once read the passage out to me, translating as she went.

From my cottage I phoned to ask if we could go through it again. Zofia said she'd dig it out and ring me back.

I heard nothing that afternoon, nor in the evening. In the morning she rang and said, 'Pheelip, I just cannot understand it. I have looked and looked and looked!'

I told her not to worry.

'No, I am like a dog with a bone when I get like this – I must chew and chew! Do you know,' she chuckled, 'I even prayed, once to Mama, and once to St Antony! I promised five pounds to the poor if it turns up. Are you sure it is not with you?'

I said I'd look, but I knew it wasn't. The following day she phoned again. 'Well done!'

'What?'

'You found the book, didn't you? It was here when I got back . . .'

The book had appeared on the chair in her room. She had sat frequently in that chair during the two days of looking. Whether it was Helena or St Antony who'd left it we couldn't decide. But whoever it was, they clearly approved of the story being told. And the poor got their five pounds.

It was 8 November 1923, a sharp autumnal day. Two farm-carts and a *bryczka* stood beneath the lime trees at Druków.

On the first cart was a pile of mattresses, trunks, jars of pickle and farm tools; Helena's bees lay among them in a sealed-up skep; a pair of Friesian cows was attached to the side of the cart. The reins of the *bryczka* were in Adam's hands;

stretched out at his feet was the retriever, Elta, with her litter of four-week-old puppies.

The second cart, drawn by Siwka and Gniadka – the two who had drawn their wedding carriage – was laid out inside with cushions and carpets. In here were Tekla and the children – Zofia wrapped in a weasel-fur hood and her brother sitting in the lap of his wet-nurse.

And beside them all, on the new mare, rode Helena: '. . . twenty-four years old, serious, excited, committed . . . I was trotting up and down along the carts as they drew away, talking to Adam, urging the maids to keep the children out of the wind . . .'

They drove all morning through the forest. In the mid afternoon the trees thinned and the bright strip of the Niemen appeared between them. They crossed the river and drove up towards the house.

Helena went on ahead. The new house had a row of five windows on each side of the porch, and a three-storey tower at one end. She dismounted and stepped inside. The air was cool and damp; it smelt of chalk and new paint. Everything was as clean and white as a hospital. The rooms were empty and the low sun stretched unbroken across the bare boards. 'We will have to find its soul,' she remembered thinking, 'we will have to find the soul of this house and fill it with voices . . .'

Outside, a small group of villagers had gathered to watch the Brońskis' arrival. With stony expressions, they ran their eyes over the contents of each cart.

Jumping down from his *bryczka*, Adam greeted them.

'Now, Panoczku,' one of them laughed, 'there'll be something to loot again!'

Helena wrote of the chill she felt on hearing this, and ended her account with this reflection:

All those early years at Mantuski we lived as if in a boiling kettle – surrounded by peasants, Germans, Bolsheviks . . . where are you headed, Poland, where are you headed?

That winter they colonized two or three rooms at the river end of the house. Adam and Bartek made some birch-wood cots, a table and a birch-wood washstand. Helena wrote, 'we lived a Cossack's life the first winter but there seemed little to worry us . . .'

One particular evening Helena recorded in her green notebook. It was mid December, and she and Adam were sitting in their makeshift dining room. A wolf-skin hung on one wall. The table was scattered with the tail-end of supper – some apples, cheese, a bowl of salted herrings, a brick of rye-bread.

Adam was talking about his day, about clearing the snow from the new barn roof, about plans to fence off the orchard in the spring, and about the shooting he had had in the Moryn wood.

'And the new sledge,' asked Helena, 'have you waxed the blades?'

'All done, *kochana!*'

The samovar purred in the corner; the wood crackled in the stove; Haust stretched out before it.

Helena stood and crossed to the window. She pulled back the curtains. The moon was nearly full. She placed one hand against the glass, and said, 'Adam, why don't we see how this new sledge works?'

Taking two large stirrup drinks, they left the house. They crossed the drive to the new, half-built stable block. The night air stung their cheeks, but there was no wind. Stretched out across the southern sky was a long cartouche of cloud, its top edge silvery in the moonlight.

On the river the snow was a sparkling white. It looked like

a long tablecloth scattered with sugar; and it was there, just inches above the Niemen, that they put the new sledge through its paces.

Helena drove. She drove upstream, heading east, towards the Russian border. The moon was a few points south of their course, but as the river arced round, the light swung across their path and came off the snow to shine in their eyes.

Adam laughed, shouting above the rush of air, 'Faster, Helutka!'

She flicked the reins, and the horses found another notch of speed. The blades sliced through the snow; the horses, their manes flapping, strained at the traces. Their hooves drummed the snow in unison and each of their movements seemed mirrored by the other.

'Aj-aj!' shouted Adam. 'These two work together like electricity!'

The river ran beside snow-covered meadows. Lips of ice hung over the bank, making cavernous spaces beneath them. The sledge dashed on, beneath the stars, between darkened fields, between stands of pine which serrated the sky, between ghost-grey birches, between the white of the river and the black of the forest.

There was an opening in the trees. The frozen Niemen ran through it and entered a wide-open plain. The sky drew back, receding to a slim horizon. Somewhere far to the north was the tiny orange glow of a fire, a jewel of colour in the colourless night.

Helena drew breath. She tugged at the reins. The horses slowed, trotting on for a while. Then the plain narrowed and the forest pressed in at the banks. She pulled at the reins again and the sledge came to a halt.

Silence. Two clouds of breath hung above the sledge. Siwka pitched her head and bellowed, and the trees and snow boxed in the sound.

Adam said, 'If we carried on we'd be in Russia by morning!'
'I know.'

Adam pulled the rug up around Helena's shoulders. For a long time they lay like that, breathing in shallow breaths, not speaking, until the cold came up between them, and they turned the horses and headed for home.

21

DURING ONE of the first winters – it is not clear which one – Helena recorded the return to Mantuski of Uncle Alek. She and Adam were alone in the new sitting room, at night, when a series of bumps sounded from the end of the house.

'Who's that, dear?' asked Helena, not looking up from the book she was reading.

Adam raised his hand, frowning. They both heard the doors in the kitchen corridor, one by one, being opened and closed. Then he smiled. 'Uncle Alek . . . It's Uncle Alek! He is back!'

Aleksander Broński was a very distant relation. He had been born in the first part of the nineteenth century, a few years after Napoleon had been chased back across the Niemen. Named after the victorious Tsar, he went on to have a distinguished military career in the Caucasus, to lead daring patrols up and down the Military Highway and during the Crimean War to hold an impossible redoubt in which he and a Greek powder-boy were the only survivors. In 1856 he retired, decorated and pensioned, and bought Mantuski.

It was Aleksander who'd built the old house. He'd knocked down a modest *dwórek*, rebuilt it, then expanded its lands and forests. He followed the usual rounds of cards and hunting and feasts, and made flying visits to St Petersburg where he drank vodka in the regimental mess and 'visited the gypsies'. Then his eye fell on a certain Russian girl, a minor heiress, from just north of the Pripet Marshes.

All one autumn he rode down there from Mantuski, twice a month, to try and persuade her to marry him.

'General Broński,' her mother told him, 'you are a man of great stature. But you are not suitable for my daughter. You are a Pole and a Catholic and have had too many mares in your stable.'

But he persisted. In January he burst into the house in a flurry of snow. He was wearing an ankle-length wolf-skin coat. The girl was alone. He threw off his coat and knelt down in front of her. Underneath the coat, he wore nothing.

'In all my nakedness,' he cried, 'I beg you to marry me!'

Having seen him like that, the poor girl felt morally bound to accept. She went to live in Mantuski. She bore Broński five children and ran his household. But it wasn't long before the old general began to rove again. He spent weeks at a time in St Petersburg and in later years brought to Mantuski, as 'governess', one of his lovers. In order that the servants would not talk, his wife was obliged to sleep in the same room, behind a Japanese screen.

It was Uncle Alek's profligate life that destined him, in the eyes of most, to haunt Mantuski. But there was another theory. In order to marry his Russian bride, Aleksander Broński had had to renounce his Catholic faith. He was buried in the Orthodox cemetery. From such a heathen place, stressed the more devout members of the family, a Broński would find it impossible to enter Heaven.

According to Zofia, Aleksander Broński was a sad ghost. He wandered the corridors of the new Mantuski, twisting door handles, shuffling across the hall, creaking on the stairs. In the hall the grandfather clock always slowed during his visits – the only time during those years that it ever faltered.

Zofia remembers seeing him sitting on the end of her bed, candle in hand, wearing his wolf-skin coat. 'He looked so miserable!' She came to dread his visits.

'We must get rid of him,' Helena had told Adam.

'Helena!'

'No, Adam. He must go. It is fair to him and fair to the children. I will write to Uncle the Bishop.'

So Uncle the Bishop came down from his see. He heaved his portly frame from room to room, with a prayer book and an aspergill; in each room he made a sign of the cross, muttered a prayer and flicked holy water onto the floor.

All through that winter, there was no sign of the ghost. Nor the following winter. Zofia slept easily. The nights were silent. And it was assumed that despite his worldly sins, his naked proposal, the adultery, the renouncing of Rome, a corner of Heaven had at last been found for poor old Uncle Alek and his wolf-skin coat.

But one morning, several years later, Helena noticed the clock had lost thirty-five minutes. That night she saw a light outside, moving among the snow-covered shrubs. She heard the creaking of the boards, and then a cry from Zofia's room. She opened the bedroom door.

'He was there, Mama, by my bed . . . Why can't he go? Why, Mama? If he's dead, why can't he go to Heaven?'

In Mantuski, Zofia and I met a lady called Pani Cichoń who lived in a new house opposite the ruins of the *dwór*. She had very red cheeks and an expression of perpetual anxiety.

'Oh yes, the ghost. They said about the ghost when we came. And you know, Pani Zofia,' her voice became a whisper, 'in the winter sometimes, there's a light there in the trees, a swinging light over there . . .' And she nodded towards the copse that had sprung out of the ruins of Mantuski.

Zofia sighed as we walked away. 'He used to carry a hurricane lamp when I saw him . . .'

So in spite of everything, the war, the burning of the house, the years of communism, it seemed as if poor old Uncle Alek had still not found a way out of his earthly wanderings.

*   *   *

In Zofia's sitting room at Braganza there is a painting of Mantuski. It was copied from a photograph and commissioned after the war. It shows the long low front, the mansard-roofed tower, the wooden porch wrapped in honeysuckle and roses. A faint chocolate-box prettiness pervades the picture. No one knew, when it was painted in 1946, that the house was already destroyed. Now it's all that's left.

One afternoon at Braganza, sitting beneath this picture, Zofia said she had found a series of notes her mother had written about the day-to-day life of Mantuski. She crossed the room and retrieved from a cupboard a file of old type-written sheets. The sheets were yellow with age and on the front of the file was written 'The Running of Mantuski':

*

In March 1924 Adam and Bartek left Mantuski for western Poland. They returned after six weeks, driving before them a dozen young Friesians and a bull. The bull had a single black marking across his back that was the exact shape of a saddle. These cattle became the base of the Mantuski dairy herd. By 1939 there were one hundred and twenty cows and sixty prime heifers. Their milk went to make cheeses, the Broński cheeses which each week were packed up in cases and taken by horse-cart to Lida, and from there to the shops of Wilno and Warsaw.

*

There were two thousand hectares of pine wood and some one thousand hectares of meadow, mostly along the Niemen. The soil was sandy and poor; that accounted for the general poverty of the villages. Oats and buckwheat were the easiest to grow, but as there was plenty of manure, they were always experimenting with new crops.

*

For the first couple of years, only enough cheese was made for the house and the *parobcy*. Helena herself made it, curdling the milk, cutting the curds into squares with a spatula, pressing them, turning them daily on shelves in a special cellar near the banks of the river.

*

The *dwór* had no electricity. Adam said that when the village has electricity, then we will too, but not before. (Electricity arrived finally at the Mantuski *kolkhoz* in 1961.)

*

The kitchen was ruled by Urszula. She spent the summer pickling cucumbers and making compote of cherry and plum and pears. She was an excellent cook, but would always complain about Helena's dogs. 'What's the use of a dog?' she'd say. 'He gives no fur, no milk, and no meat.'

*

Helena planted the orchards in 1924. They grew very quickly. Apple trees, pear trees, cherry trees, and among them the beehives brought from Druków. She also planted the larch at this time [the larch that alone survived the war and had directed us to the ruins of the house]. There were greenhouses full of tomatoes, even melons. Each Wednesday Waldek took the surplus to market in Iwje and returned with salt, paraffin, petrol, and 'colonial' products like sugar and coffee.

*

Mantuski had a carpenter and a blacksmith. Between them they made all the carts and carriages, and much of the furniture in the early years. Iron bars would come in each winter from Lida to be smelted and beaten into stove doors, harness-buckles and nails. The blacksmith was a tall and solemn man who kept to himself and was said to have second sight.

*

Horses. Mantuski was famous for its horses. Each of the *parobcy* was in charge of two work-horses. Helena offered a large cash bonus for the best-kept pair. She used to be horrified by the skeletal animals she saw on other estates. It was the health of the Mantuski horses, said Zofia, that saved them in 1939.

*

There were always books in the house, brought down in parcels from Wilno. Books in French and English, German and Polish. Weekly newspapers came too, and in later years a copy of the *Revue de Deux Mondes* which arrived from Paris by subscription, and sat on a round wooden table in the library. This, added Zofia, was the paper that always prompted the most interesting discussions.

*

After the spring flood in April the herd was taken out to graze the meadows. They left the byres each morning after the 4 a.m. milking. The churns were driven out to the meadows for the noon milking, the milk-maids sitting on the carts. Immediately afterwards the milk was separated, part of it put aside for the house, the calves and the *parobcy*, the rest used for cheese.

*

In the summer, Helena swam every morning in the river. After breakfast she did her 'rounds', riding to the cheese factory, the byres, visiting the sick in the village.

*   *   *

Helena's relationship with the land characterizes her papers of this time more than anything else. When she spoke of the land it was always with passion, even ecstasy. Yet in 1933 she could write this:

The loneliness of Mantuski! It is no joke. No one comes in winter. No kindred spirit to talk to. No one to consult. Adam is always away, and when he comes back on Sundays there are always queues and queues of people waiting to see him. I am still young and used to social life and theatre and conversation. And all there is around are villages of Belorussian peasants who resent us. I am responsible for every human being and every animal in the immediate area, for solving every problem. The icy, white, silent solitude of these winters, the unending cruel winters. They have broken me, and I feel constantly ill and unhappy . . .

Several years later, she offered a more measured appraisal:

In these last years I have learned to manage Mantuski. I have learned to deal with the people. Everything has gone happily, smoothly and easily. In 1937–38, the estate has gone from strength to strength, become prosperous. I am now happy when alone there, more than happy, surrounded by love and friends. Tamed human beings, tamed animals.

And that is the impression that remains. Despite the 'boiling kettle', the frustrations and hardships, the murmurings in the villages, Mantuski was Helena's life. The years before were a prelude. The land, the house, her new family, the new Poland were all linked in a dense coincidence of renewal and growth that swelled through the years of the 1920s. And only towards the end and in her darker moments did she admit that they were, all of them, living on borrowed time.

Zofia herself has several very clear memories of the first years at Mantuski.

In the first a governess is putting her to bed. The governess is telling her she must always sleep with her hands above the blanket. Above the blanket! Like that! This puzzled Zofia and she asked why. To prevent unclean to-does! But it merely meant her hands became cold. She put them under the blanket as soon as the governess had gone. It all made very little sense.

The second image is of the arrival of her first pony. Zofia is having her hair washed. She sees the pony through the window and runs outside with her hair streaming and dripping behind her. She jumps on and canters round and round the lawn beneath the larch. The pony is very small; it is named Karmelek, which means 'toffee'.

The third memory is the earliest. She is lying in a pram beneath some sort of arbour. It is autumn and the leaves are falling all around her; they fall on to the pram, into the hood, all about her head – papery chestnut leaves swinging down from the sky.

'You know,' she told me, 'whenever I think of Mantuski it always has this underwater feeling to it. Those leaves like flat stones sinking in a river . . . Everything submerged in greenery, those enormous limes, everything in slow motion . . .'

One more scene came back to Zofia from those early years. She was standing near the larch in front of the house. She was about nine or ten. The gardener's son came across the lawn. He hit the trunk of the larch with a stick, then said, 'You know where babies come from?'

'Yes,' said Zofia.

'Where?'

'Storks,' she answered. 'Storks bring them in their beaks from Africa.'

The gardener's son laughed. 'You think so?'

She nodded weakly.

'It's nonsense!'

'Well, where then?'

'You really want to know?'

'Yes.'

'Sure?'

'Yes.'

He leaned over to whisper in her ear. She could feel his cupped hand against her cheek, his breath warm on her skin.

'Oj-oj!' she exclaimed.

'It's true! I've seen it myself!'

Zofia frowned. 'How much does it cost?'

'A hundred zlotys for a maid. Three hundred for a boy.'

She found it hard to imagine. What an extraordinary picture! But, she reasoned, it was no less plausible than storks. She cursed the governess who'd fed her that fable and for years afterwards believed there really was an old woman who sold babies in Iwje market.

22

IN JULY OF 1925, Adam was offered the post of judge in Iwje. It meant spending most of the week away from Mantuski but, as he said in a letter to Helena, 'By judging I can earn enough to put Mantuski back on its feet. Five hundred zlotys a month is a good salary!'

And from then on, Adam always lived away from Mantuski, returning at weekends and only occasionally for periods of a few weeks.

Zofia has a photograph of her father at about this time. He is reclining in some long grass, in shirt-sleeves and tie. Zofia is leaning against his knee. He has small eyes and a large head and the scale of him and his wide-open expression give him a look of outsize benevolence.

His letters confirm the impression. They are full of an apparent delight at all things. In 1924 he had written to Helena during one of her trips to Wilno:

> 15 April. Mantuski.
> Helena, my love!
> The last few days have been beautiful. The ice is cracking on the Niemen and you can see the water bubbling beneath it. Spring is on its way! We have started fencing. Tomorrow we begin to milk three times a day . . . The cows are expecting, the horses are expecting, and there are a dozen little chicks squeaking like cartwheels in the hen house! I am looking for stove tiles in some of the old sheds. But everything seems broken or vanished.

We had three days of cloud and rain earlier this week, with hailstones like peas. And now – a lovely April day. Not a cloud. I rode out through the fields. I heard the first clucking of the heathercock. The larks are screaming in the heavens. Soon we will start planting potatoes. I feel as fit as a fiddle, my love, as healthy as a fish in the Niemen, a capercaillie on the branch, a wolf in the marsh!

I have collected the roses and we can plant them at once – they are splendid specimens, great long roots! . . . How healthy the horses look now – I remember what they were like after the war – ugh! Surely, Hela, things are getting better on earth. The world is speeding towards happiness . . .

Adam always kept a close eye on what was happening in Warsaw, and was keen on discussing affairs of state. Where Helena was a pragmatist, he was an optimist; where she railed against the corruption of the Sejm, he remained convinced it would all work out. 'Time, Hela dear. You can't break in a horse overnight. Poland is no more than a skittish young colt!'

Yet since the election in 1921, he had watched the Polish parliament fragment, year by year, into a mosaic of squabbling factions. Minister replaced minister, cabinet replaced cabinet; and each one proved more impotent than the last.

Adam followed the comings and goings, the coalitions, the broken coalitions, the flaccid promises, with a growing sense of disappointment. Perhaps Helena was right. This was not the Poland he had fought for. Around him, in the villages, he sensed a gathering resentment among the Belorussians; in court his own authority was sometimes shaky. Mutterings of nationalism, from all sides, grew louder.

In May 1926 Marshal Piłsudski became weary of the bickering. Deciding to rein in the skittish young colt, he emerged from retirement, marched on the Sejm in Warsaw, and sacked it. One thousand people died in the fighting. Though the Marshal declined the presidency, the centre managed, by his intervention, to reassert its authority. A policy of *sanacja* – 'regenerative purge' – was set against the *partyjnictwo* – 'party corruption and chaos'.

In Kresy, the summer of 1926 came early. News of Piłsudski's coup reached Mantuski with the first dust-clouds, kicked up by timber carts in the village street. In the still air, the lilac hung limply on its panicled stalks; the sand-martins flew to and fro above the Niemen.

It was hot; still and hot and airless. Dogs lay all day in the shade, loping from shadow to shadow as the sun passed overhead. Jewels of resin swelled from the cabins' weather boards; the nights were close and heavy.

Shortly after St Antony's day, on yet another hot June morning, Bartek appeared shiny-faced and hatless in the doorway of Adam's office in Iwje.

'Trouble, Pan Adam.'

'What trouble, Bartek?'

'The villagers, Pan Adam. They've blocked the timber carts. They say the trees we're felling's theirs. Say it was you that gave them, sir.'

'Which trees are they?'

'Up behind the crossways. 'Tween there and the church.'

'But I gave them the woodland above that!'

Adam cursed. He stared for a moment at Bartek. Then he looked away, at the oblong of light that pierced his office, at the town square beyond. He picked up his hat and led Bartek back to the street.

On the edge of Mantuski village, the issue had already been decided. The timber workers, their path blocked, had backed away from the militant villagers, taking fright at the armoury of forks and flails waved at them. They'd returned to the *dwór* steadings. The villagers now sat in a triumphant group. One or two lay on the bank, hats pulled down over their eyes. A group of young men sat in the shade talking heatedly about their victory to the *wójt*, the elected village head.

The *wójt* stood up at the approach of Adam's *bryczka*. He was an elderly, quiet-spoken man. Adam had always found him fair-minded and believed the two of them shared the same deep love of the land.

The *wójt* put his hand on the wheel-rim and leaned forward towards Adam.

'This is not of my choosing, Pan Adam. It's of politics.'

'What can we do?'

'I have spoken all I can and they will not move. It's the younger ones with their ideas.'

Adam climbed down from the *bryczka* and approached the group. The core of young men elbowed themselves up and looked at him blankly.

Adam stood before them. 'I have given you the woodland beyond the church and the meadows. This wood here belongs to the *dwór*.'

The row of stubbly chins remained motionless. Flies buzzed around their faces. There was silence.

Adam paused, looking at each of them in turn. 'Tomorrow morning, I will bring the carts back to this wood and I expect to be allowed through. If again you resist, I will be obliged to summon the authorities from Nowogródek.'

In the morning they were still there. Adam spoke briefly to the *wójt*, then went with him to the exchange to telephone Nowogrudek.

The district commissioner was a retired major from the Polish cavalry. The Belorussian cause held little weight with him; he had applauded Piłsudski's coup. He growled at Adam down the telephone: 'I will be in Mantuski by noon.'

Adam met him by the ferry. Four constables rode beside

him. Each of them had a rifle in a pouch behind his saddle.

It was not the first such show of strength the district commissioner had dealt with. He was very clinical. He read a statement, demanding the villagers to move.

They stayed put.

He warned them that if they did not move, he would order his constables to fire over their heads.

They did not move.

He ordered his men to dismount. They loaded their weapons and knelt in a short line. 'Fire!'

The shots rang out around the forest. A group of rooks rose croaking from the lime trees. The villagers bunched together a little, but none broke ranks.

The *wójt* stepped out in front of the commissioner, and approached the militants. He started arguing with them; the group loosened its bonds. The *wójt* came over and announced they would let the carts through.

Adam asked, 'What did you say, *wójt*?'

'I spoke plain, Pan Adam. I said if you want to die for the sake of a few trees, that's well and good, but think of your kin.'

For several weeks after this, wrote Helena, Adam brooded. She had never seen him so withdrawn, so *piano*. His spirits returned but his unbridled optimism did not. And in the coming years, she heard more and more talk from him of land reform.

In court, Helena said, Adam could be quite stern. After 1926, he became particularly hard on what he called crimes of *nienawiść*, of bitterness, either between *szlachta* and peasants, or between Belorussian and Pole. His summing-ups, all the more striking for coming from a gentle man, left quite a mark on the convicted. But somehow his sentencing never impressed the Polish authorities.

In the summer of 1927 a woman of about nineteen was brought before him by the sheriff. She wore a pale calico dress. Her thin arms hung loosely from it, trailing like withies at her hips. Coffee-drop freckles were scattered over her nose, and she had very large eyes, like a rabbit's. She was called Tessa Stanicka, and was accused of attempted murder.

'Was my baby, sir.'

'Your baby? You tried to kill your baby?'

'Yes, sir. Yes, your honour.'

Adam was unused to such speedy confessions. 'Why did you try to kill your baby, Tessa Stanicka?'

'I never asked for the baby, sir. I never wanted 'ee.'

'And what did you do to him?'

'I put him on the tip, sir, at night. Under cabbage leaves. But the priest, Father Jerzy, he came to see my mother on 'count of 'er terrible illness in the morning, sir, and his 'orse was nibbling the cabbage leaves and there was the little baby still warm and 'live, sir, when His Reverence came in the morning . . .'

The clerk had difficulty keeping up with her admission, and raised a hand for her to pause.

'So you don't deny it?'

'Oh no, sir!'

'Even though it is a serious crime, and carries a stiff sentence.'

'Well, sir, the way I see it is that if you commits a crime, it's what happens.'

Adam nodded. 'And where is the child now?'

'An orphanage, your honour sir.'

'And you realize you cannot see the child?'

'Like I said, I never asked for 'ee.'

Adam looked across the courtroom at her. Her rabbit eyes blinked in his gaze. He could see nothing in them: neither fear nor remorse nor evil.

'Tessa Stanicka, you have committed not only a grave crime

against the state, but a sin against God. You were given the gift of a child and you squandered it like a runt piglet. Would you do it again?'

'No, sir.'

'How can we be sure?'

'I don't 'ave another baby, sir. I don't want one.'

'No —' Adam was thrown for a moment by her logic. He carried on. 'However, I do not detect in you any malice and feel that with the right circumstances, you will be able to live a virtuous life. Do you think that is possible, Tessa?'

'Oh yes, sir!'

'And you are sorry for what you did?'

'Oh yes, sir!'

Adam summoned the sheriff and asked him, in hushed tones, about her family.

'Her mother has disowned her,' whispered the sheriff. 'If she goes back to her village they will starve her to death.'

Adam tapped his fingers on the oak table. Then he leaned towards the girl and said, 'Tell me, Tessa, have you ever worked in service?'

When, several days later, Adam returned to Mantuski with Tessa, and announced she was to be a maid, Helena was incredulous. 'Among our own children, Adam? How could you employ this murderess!'

But Tessa took quickly to her new role. In time she proved the best of all Helena's maids. Others came and went, lured to the altar or to the city, but Tessa showed no interest in anything but keeping birds – hawfinches, chaffinches, goldfinches which flocked to her window like disciples. She remained at Mantuski, perpetually naive, perpetually loyal, loved with an unquestioning love by the children and surrounded by an ever-growing choir of passerine song.

Helena loved that birdsong. It took her back to St Petersburg, to Liki the Chinese songbird and Aunt Ziuta and the smell of herring on snowy street corners, to the astrakhan hats in Gostinny Dvor; and to the sight of her father, frail and smiling by the Moika Canal, leaning on an ivory-topped cane and reciting a couplet from Mickiewicz.

By the end of the 1920s, wrote Helena, Mantuski was 'back on its feet'. Yields had grown steadily and cheeses were now being sent for sale to Wilno, to Warsaw and Cracow. The house no longer looked new and spartan but was alive – alive with the three children, alive with dogs; the larch in front of the house had grown level with the eaves.

Yet it was still a harsh life and there was frequent illness. One autumn, when she was about eight or nine, Zofia's brother developed a sudden temperature and when it dropped back, he started to cough up blood. The doctor came after three days and told Helena that the child stood little chance of seeing out the winter – unless she could be taken south, to France or Italy.

There being no money for such a trip at Mantuski, Adam spoke to his father. Stanisław Broński had little truck with rest-cures.

'Children,' he told Adam, 'they're like glasses! If one breaks, you simply get another.'

Helena's Uncle Nicholas was more accommodating. He put up the money and Helena took Tessa and the children to a small villa in Juan-les-Pins. With the help of a very kind Belgian doctor, Zofia's brother recovered and in early March the party journeyed back across Europe, each of the children parcelled up in a set of brand-new linen clothes, with a spray of freckles on their teak-brown noses.

The illness had shaken Helena. She had seen the French hospitals, the new drugs and the surgery. Eastern Poland seemed medieval by comparison. Dogged as she was by her own ill health, she told Adam she would set up a clinic for the village.

'But Hela, you know nothing of such things!'

She explained that she had once studied nursing in Wilno. He looked sceptical.

But for the most part it proved enough. The ailments that the villagers brought to Helena were simple ones. Anything serious they left to prayer, or the magic of roaming quacks.

Twice a week, she opened the side door of the house and villagers would come into a small back room that she had labelled: MANTUSKI KLINIKA. At the beginning they came mainly out of curiosity, peering at the jars in the glass-fronted cupboards, at the kidney-shaped basins and steel scissors, at Helena in her white coat. The women of the village remained wary of her powers, but the men soon became fond of the swish of Helena's lye-starched coat, and the touch of her scrubbed hands on their skin.

She had a small repertoire of remedies, to match the small repertoire of ailments. She devised a barley poultice for lumbago, a lime and honey balsam for colds and sore throats. She dabbed iodine on burns. For flesh wounds she raided the dairy for fresh unsalted butter and, with a few herbs, made a dressing with lint obtained from ravelled linen. As a sudorific, she used extract of dried raspberries. For the 'three-day ague', a common Mantuski complaint, she gave a course of quinine. She refused, outright, requests for 'them leeches' to flush out the 'dark blood' and kept a store of placebos – herb and cream ointments and infusions. She was quite fierce with time wasters, and particularly short with a Pani Kasia who once a month brought her cat to be cured of 'his fearful downcast spirit'.

23

FROM THE BEGINNING of the year 1933, Helena's day-to-day diaries have survived. They continue intermittently until the outbreak of the war.

1933 it seems was a trying year, a yo-yo type of a year, with wild swings of mood and fortune. The spring was late. Planting fell behind. May and June were very wet. Then came July, clear and warm and perfect for mowing. Open canoes crossed the Niemen laden with hay. The barn doors were thrown open; lines of rack wagons creaked through the village towards them. It was a record cut.

On 11 July Helena recorded:

> What brilliant days! The whole world simply bursting with activity, silver scythes shimmer in the meadows, the cherries better than ever. The house is full of warmth and sun . . . Adam here for the weekend and I am madly madly happy with him around. He is so good, so loyal, so thoughtful and incredibly kind. I adore him more with each year that passes. We have more and more in common. I miss him so terribly in the weeks . . .

On Sundays Adam and Helena would have lunch at a large table by the river. They grilled bream or a Niemen jackfish and sometimes as many as fourteen would gather around that table – the three children, visiting cousins, Uncle Nicholas, Helena's ageing mother, Panna Konstancja from Wilno, the new governess from Grodno.

For a while everything fell into place: milk yields were up, the cheeses recovered their distinctive pre-war flavour, and the buckwheat and rye, free of witch grass, blew like silk in the July breeze.

Then a number of things happened. First the governess from Grodno was found swimming at night with one of the married *parobcy*. Helena asked her to leave and she locked herself in her room. For nearly two days she refused to come out. Bartek had to prise off her door and the last they saw of the Grodno governess she was lying on her bed, being driven to the station on the back of a farm cart.

In August Smok, Helena's favourite prize bull, became ill. She sat up all night with him, dabbing his sweating flanks with a solution of soap and whey.

Then in September, she watched four unfamiliar carts pull up in the yard. A young Jewish merchant from Iwje jumped down: he said he had come for the Mantuski hay. Adam had offered it as surety on a loan to someone he hardly knew.

Helena was furious. She sent a letter to Adam with the merchants. She told him she'd give them only two carts of hay; the rest he was to make up with his own cash; if her cows went hungry that winter, she added, she would divorce him.

By the end of the summer, Helena made the following entry:

> Endless trouble with this place! Smok, my dear red-and-white, is now dying. Another bull, Paw, is dead. The cows are forever ill. Adam drops in now and again, hates to listen to the problems, gives non-sensical orders, lets the *parobcy* use the horses for whatever they want, leaves me with an absolute mess and departs. It is pouring with rain. Stefania the laundry girl is ill. There is no linen. It is enough to make you weep or go crazy . . .

By Christmas of 1933, with the winter weaving its slow web across the land, the running of Mantuski had calmed. It was

clear there would be enough hay; the cows would not starve;
Helena forgot all about divorce:

> Life is peaceful here, restful, comfortable. Adam is
> back from Iwje and the house is again full of his high
> spirits. We are affectionate together. He plays games
> with the children. If only he were here more often!
> Late last night we sat and watched the moon and
> talked. How lucky I am to have such love! Skating
> has started on the river and skiing. I adore a life of
> sport . . .

On Christmas Day both Adam and Zofia became ill. Zofia was
much the worse. Within two days, her temperature had risen
to 103° and she was delirious. The doctor said it was scarlet
fever.

'But she's had scarlet fever!' protested Helena.

'She has it again,' he said. 'It can happen.'

For two days, Helena sat with Zofia while she writhed around
and talked nonsense and sweated. On day three her temperature
fell back a little and the whole family moved up to Wilno.
Adam's illness, no more than a cold, passed quickly.

At this time, the children were all at school in Wilno. Adam
had been appointed director of a bank in the town and the
family, during term-time, rented a flat that overlooked the
Wilja river.

The Wilja was frozen throughout January and there was
skating in the fields below Three Crosses Hill. One Sunday in
early February, they were all returning from Mass. Bright sun
bounced off the snow in the park and lit up their faces. Zofia
and her brothers were walking behind their parents. Suddenly
Adam shuffled to a stop. He sat down on a bench and looked
wordlessly at Helena. After a minute or two, he said he could
continue, but the following day Helena urged him to see a
doctor.

He returned to the flat at four in the afternoon. He sat down heavily in a chair in Helena's dressing room. He too, it seemed, had had scarlet fever and it had 'reached his heart'. The doctor told him he must have a complete rest.

Helena was horrified. She imagined him being unable to shoot, unable to play tennis. She begged him to go to bed. 'Please, please, please,' she sobbed, invoking every saint she could think of for him to take care, to go south to the Krynica spa.

Adam took her hands. 'Only now, *kochana*, do I understand that you really love me!'

'You know I adore you! But please, please look after your health! Go to Krynica!'

The next day they went to order him a new suit for the south. She made him promise to write every day, and to do what the doctors said. They called on the specialist. He had seen the latest x-rays and he shook his head: Adam could make no journey. The x-rays showed his heart horribly enlarged.

He went to bed in the flat. The room looked over the river. Helena read to him, from *The Story of San Michele* and *Edouard VII et son temps*. They played halma and chess. Slowly he improved and by March they were able to go out, taking a droshky to the forest wrapped in furs. But Helena said there was now a strange blankness in his eyes. She went back to talk to the specialist, alone.

'What is happening, doctor?'

The doctor shifted awkwardly in his chair. She repeated the question.

He picked up a pencil and said, 'If death is Warsaw, Madame Brońska, then the train is just leaving Wilno.'

Back at the flat, the afternoon sun filled the rooms with its orange light. Helena said nothing to Adam. She herself refused to understand what the doctor had said, what they all knew. Adam sat listlessly in a chair. They talked of Mantuski. They trod every corner of the land, inspected every building and wood; they stalked the capercaillie, swam in the Niemen, and she refused his tacit admission that he would see none of it again.

'I will leave you Mantuski,' he said.

'Nonsense!' Helena took his hand. 'You will weep at my funeral and then go out and marry that Zboromirska!'

Pani Zboromirska was a young widow who always became animated when she saw Adam. Helena ordered flowers to be sent to him and signed them 'Zboromirska'. She dabbed water on the card to make it look like tears. Adam believed it; bashfully he pretended they had come from an aunt.

That was Holy Week. His room was full of flowers. The children came to see him twice a day; their Palm Sunday osiers were pinned to the wall. A ruff of newspapers lay below the bed. Helena had come in late on Easter night to check his pulse and he had opened his eyes.

'Helena, my dear.'

She lay with him that time, the last time, terrified in case he should be hurt. But afterwards he fell asleep and slept while she listened for his breaths, waiting for each one as it fell from his lips, collecting them. His face was placid like an icon.

She rose slowly to prevent him waking and in the darkness crossed to the window. Far below, the river shone silver-grey in the moonlight.

'Pantarei,' she muttered. 'All things pass.'

'Pantarei,' she repeated, weeks later, watching the Niemen through the window at Mantuski, while the teardrops fell into her coffee. 'Pantarei . . .'

Zofia was alone in the Wilno house. She was twelve, sitting on her bed, doing her homework. There was a sudden noise through the partition. She rushed into her father's room.

'He was struggling for breath. I held his hand and spoke to

him but he could not hear. There was just this noise from his throat. I picked up the phone and rang the doctor but he didn't answer. He lived only two stops on the bus so I ran out of the house and ran for the bus which was pulling away. I remember the conductor saying: "Careful, little one! You'll give yourself a heart attack with all that running!" I found the doctor and we hurried home but of course, Papa was already dead.

'In his room were dozens and dozens of hyacinths; to this day I cannot see hyacinths without thinking of his death.'

Adam was buried several days later, at the family chapel near Nowogródek. It was a grey, breezy morning. Uncle the Bishop stood over the grave. The wind came through the pines and scuffed the pages of his Bible. Before the coffin was closed, Helena placed on Adam's chest the pocket-knife he had given her in 1915, and a letter. She copied the letter:

> Goodbye, *moj ptaszyku*. Goodbye, my dearest heart.
> I shall look after your children as you would wish
> and I shall be brave. I will make you proud of me.
> May God bless you, my love, and may the soil rest
> lightly on you. Thank you for what you have been
> to me. God will help me. I shall love you always.
> Be at peace, my dear one, be at peace . . .

*

1992. Nowogródek. Zofia wanted to find her father's grave. She was very tired. I suggested she wait, but she said no, she must get it over with.

We drove through dripping forests. The unmetalled road was deserted. A darkness hung over everything.

'I remember the chapel,' she said. 'The family chapel on a kind of low hill . . .'

We pulled out of the trees and the road passed between a pair of rye fields. It was still raining. Beyond the fields, perhaps half a mile beyond, the dark green of the forest closed in again. To the left was a small knoll. 'Yes, look.'

It was a larch, like the larch that marked the ruins of Mantuski – another larch rising above the hazel bushes. Beside it was the chapel.

It was still standing, though in a poor state. We left the car and walked up towards it. One of four columns had collapsed and the roof had buckled and fallen in.

Adam's grave was outside. An iron railing ran around the plot. Inside the railing was an empty hole. The grave had been ransacked.

A small group of villagers had gathered to watch us. The rain dripped from their hats. It was during the war, they said, during the war – bandits . . . partisans . . . the treasure, for the rings and the gold teeth . . .

Zofia stood there for several minutes; she was unable to speak. She stared into the darkness of her father's grave. 'It's all upside down, Pheelip, this whole terrible world is upside down. When we come here to the grave, it's come back up to earth, and when we go to our house it's buried itself under the ground. It's all upside down . . .'

24

FOR ALL OF THAT SUMMER, the summer of 1934, Helena remained at Mantuski. A stream of visitors flowed through the house. They all had their advice, and imparted it: Uncle the Bishop with his whispered devotions, Helena's mother ('Your dog's duty is to the children'), Panna Konstancja ('that Dame Cross-bones!'), Uncle Nicholas ('It is us who are now the next row for felling').

Helena carried on. She carried on mechanically. She rose each morning, dressed, spent time with the children, checked the stables, checked the cows, checked the cheese-making. She trod Mantuski's dusty summer soil like a ghost. She passed from the smells of the stables, to the clanging pails at milking, to the cool of the house at midday. But, by her own account, she felt nothing, heard nothing, smelt nothing.

July was impossibly hot. The cattle wallowed in the shallows, up to their knees in mud. In the yellow desert of the afternoon, too bright to work, Helena walked and swam, clutching hopelessly at the fringes of her old life.

On one day in August, skirting the fallows, she looked back over the dry tangle of witch grass. She looked over the fur of rye; she felt herself merge with the heat-haze, rising up like the mist, spinning like a dust-devil. She closed her eyes and tilted her head up and it was orange again, like the Wilja river, like the room in which Adam had died, in which they were engaged – orange like the day in 1914 when she'd lain beneath the birch boughs at Klepawicze, the day the war had begun and the walls of her first world had fallen.

*   *   *

With the first cool of autumn, Helena returned to earth. There was a small fire that damaged one of the barns. She took delivery of a new bull. Plough-shares peeled away the stubble and the top layer of soil, and the winter rye was drilled in. A new governess arrived from Warsaw.

Helena knew that her mother was right; her 'dog's duty' was to her children. She wrote out a list of resolutions:

1. Pray against negative thoughts (worse than evil thoughts).
2. Be outwardly gay and serene.
3. Pray for Adam, pray for the children.
4. Talk to every member of the household, visit the village.
5. Do not complain.
6. Stay busy! Walk, ride, swim whenever possible.

One day in early October, she rode out along the banks of the Niemen. Brushing aside a clutch of birch branches, she entered the forest. There was still a little birdsong and for a moment she was transported by it. She felt the familiar fusion of the senses, the feeling the forest always brought her, and knew that here at least, here among the trees, she could be assured of solace. Then she heard the tok-tok of an axe. It was Sunday: there should be no felling.

She rode towards the noise and in a clearing came across three men beside a freshly felled birch.

'What are you doing?' she demanded. 'This is *dwór* timber.'

One of the men looked up at her briefly before resuming his work. 'The *dwór* has no master now.'

'I am in charge of the *dwór*!'

The man swung his axe and it lodged in the bole of another birch. He worked it free. 'Mantuski's no place for a woman alone.'

'Nothing's changed!'

The man let his axe fall to his side. He looked up at Helena again but said nothing.

'If you need wood for fuel,' she said, 'come to the *dwór*. We have plenty now. But I will not have this cowardly stealing!'

The man smiled faintly. There was a trace of pity in his face. He called away his men, and there was no more stealing.

Isolation crept up on Helena like a mute stranger. Winter was tolerable, but in the summer, that second summer after Adam's death, she felt the first whispers of madness.

'Work,' she told herself. 'I must bury myself in work.' And she smiled to herself: Adam had always called such remedies 'the refuge of Calvinists'.

She spent her time working on an elaborate plan for replanting the forests. In Wilno she discovered a certain variety of Russian plum and planted a new orchard. She bought two new beehives, swam in the mornings, walked in the evenings, went to Mass; and there were evenings when for a whole hour she managed to forget.

But in early September she met a doctor in Lida who examined the dark smudges beneath her eyes and said, 'Madame Brońska, you are suffering from nervous exhaustion.'

He recommended a spa. Karlsbad, he said, a very civilized spa. She travelled there by train and took a room in a hotel with high ceilings and clanging pipes. Karlsbad survived in her imagination – from a visit years before with her mother – in two random scenes: the matchbox town viewed from a dangling funicular cabin, and a goat she'd watched near the hotel, chewing its way through the pages of a Bible.

The dining room at her hotel was full of guests at pink-clothed tables, eating alone. There were aspidistras by the door and cascades of rococo plasterwork. In the evenings an ice swan perched on the buffet table.

During the day, she sat on the terrace. She sipped spa water and watched Europe's leisured hordes drift past her table: the spruce Germans, the Czechs, the Austrians, the Swedes and, a little apart from them all, the Jews and the English with their look of private detachment.

Helena loved being alone in a place where everyone else was alone. She felt somehow better at it than those around her. She received steam baths in the morning and, after a week, a proposal of marriage from a moustachioed Parisian lawyer. She said no, she had children, and a house in Poland – but for days afterwards she felt a tight knot in her chest like a stone.

One afternoon she walked up into the mountains. She passed the last station of the funicular and she pressed on into the forest. It was nearing dusk; there was no one about. The evening was full of the first dusty smells of autumn. A hare bolted across her path and she paused to look down a narrow ravine, to where the 'V' of the slopes opened out into a vast, dark expanse of tree-tops. How she missed Mantuski! She thought of the children, the byres and the cheese factory, and the dampness on the banks of the river and the last autumn two years ago with Adam.

Looking up, she saw her path double back up the slope. A rock bounced down through the undergrowth. She noticed the figure of a man in a long, bottle-green coat walking quickly down the path towards her. They met on the corner. She could see his head, bald and globular in the semi-darkness. She prepared to greet him, then saw as he turned that he was wearing a black velvet mask; only his eyes and his lips appeared through it.

Helena was too shocked to move. The man stood before her. She watched him slip both hands inside his coat. Opening it, he suddenly revealed the pale folds of his flesh. He panted something in a bestial German – then lunged at her. He pushed her back against the trunk of a pine, fumbled with her clothes, pressed hard against her with his hips. And all the time, inches from her face, the mask leered at her without moving.

She tried to wriggle away. The material of his green coat was rough against her cheek. He took one hand from her shoulder and she ducked violently; the man stumbled, and she was free.

She ran. She ran back down the hill, past the funicular station. In the hotel she went to her room and drew a bath; she felt as if her very skin were a thick layer of dirt and spent a long time in the water, scrubbing and scrubbing.

Two days later she saw the bottle-green coat again, crossing one of the cobbled squares. On its arm was a Czech woman whom Helena had been talking to in the hotel. Her husband had also died recently.

'Widowhood', she had confided to Helena, 'is not something one wants to endure for too long.'

Helena was in the forest, not far from Mantuski village, on a day in spring that had broken free of its early frost to bring the first real warmth of the year. She was walking with a local woman and talking about dogs, books and the ceaseless trials of life.

The Russian Woman, as she was known, was said to be the illegitimate child of a White Russian general. She had arrived in Mantuski after the war and married a taciturn woodman. The villagers were vaguely suspicious of her sudden appearance and never called her anything but the Russian Woman. But she had a passionate, sage-like presence and many – including Helena – learnt to rely on her words in times of crisis. Beneath her scarf was a crown of sand-blonde hair and eyes of a remarkable pale brown.

In the same month as Adam had died in Wilno, the Russian Woman's taciturn woodman had been found frozen upright in a ditch near the Niemen. He had been there for two days. His arm rose out of a deep snowdrift, stretching for the birch root that would have freed him.

'No,' said the Russian Woman quietly. 'I'll never be married again.'

'How can you say never?'

She shrugged.

'But we were not meant to live alone!'

'I do not believe that, Pani Helena. I see my own suffering and joy as too great now to share with anyone but God.'

'And what does God do with those things?'

The Russian Woman glanced at Helena. 'Don't lose your faith. Never lose faith.'

How such advice infuriated her! She had heard it from a dozen priests; she had heard it from her Uncle the Bishop. She knew they were right, and this infuriated her still more.

In the autumn of 1936, Helena's mother came to stay. Poor Mama! Helena now always thought of her mother as 'Poor Mama', this frail woman who spoke about nothing but Poland's great families – Radziwiłłs, Potockis, Zamoyskis – and read only early mystics – Teresa of Avila, St John of the Cross, Thomas à Kempis. At Mantuski she spent her days in a leather chair by the window. She squinted at the river, pressing Helena to get married again.

Helena's mother lived in constant fear of the Russians coming. In Wilno, where she kept a large flat, she sought out the reassuring company of priests and colonels. Her friends and family had proved a disappointment. She had finally fallen out with Aunt Anna, who had left Poland for South America and a Jewish composer.

Helena tried all she could to cheer up her mother. She arranged bridge parties and lunches and staged a series of Gospel sketches performed by the children. But it all washed over her.

Only when she started to involve her in the workings of the farm did she show any interest at all. Helena ran through the books, the milk yields, the cheese-making, the timber felling, discussed the planting rotas, the feeds, wages, new machinery.

One afternoon with the sky low and steely grey, Helena wrapped her mother in furs and took her to see the herd. The cows were stalled for the winter. One end of the byre had just been extended, with plans to add another twenty or so heifers from the spring calves. The new stalls were empty – except for the last one, a larger one, in which stood the dozing form of Goliath.

Goliath had replaced Smok as Mantuski's bull. He had come as a frisky red-and-white calf and had swelled, under an experimental diet of beet and vitamins, to an enormous size. His markings were a deep copper and he had fluffy white hair around his eyes and a whirlpool of it that spun around his forehead. He stood in his stall like some great ship in dry dock.

The old woman leaned on the rail, patted his haunch, and smiled for the first time in weeks. Helena felt a glow of filial pride.

From somewhere far up the shed came a slow bovine groan, and Goliath snorted.

'Careful, Mama!' cried Helena. Goliath threw up his head and turned, backing his rump against the rail. There was a rattling of metal and a straining of wood. Helena's mother stepped backwards. Her foot caught in the drain and she fell, twisting, to the stone floor. Her head flopped harmlessly into some straw. But her leg was locked at a strange angle.

'Jesus, Mary!' she hissed. 'I cannot move.'

With the help of Bartek and a cow hand, they transported her to the Klinika in a barrow. 'Them new stalls,' said the cow hand. 'I knew they was bad, Pani Brońska – they'd been neither blessed nor tallowed!'

Helena's mother had broken her leg. They set it in a splint. She was sent to the station on a bed of straw. In Wilno, she had the leg set and in three months' time she was walking. But she never went to Mantuski again.

In the village, the news spread quickly. Such an accident was clearly not chance, and the consensus was that something was amiss.

The cow-hand was partly right: the correct procedure had not been followed before the beast was installed. No prayer had been said at the new threshold, no broom or hatchet buried in the foundations. It was either the building that was at fault, or the bull.

Reluctantly Helena called a priest to bless the extended byre and the various objects and amulets that were now secreted beneath it.

But the following spring, a strange disease spread through the herd and four cows, with their unborn calves, died in quick succession. The *parobcy* began to mutter darkly about a 'bad bull'. They would not go near Goliath. Unable to sell him, Helena was forced to have him butchered.

25

AT THE END OF MAY 1937, the priest of Mantuski – Orthodox and Belorussian – was found with a home-made bomb. His plan, he confessed, had been to blow up the *dwór*. He was removed by the Polish authorities.

That summer Helena became more and more aware of what she called 'the menacing atmosphere'. On a hot July morning, she was walking the dogs across the lawn when Gregory the ferryman came running up the drive. He stopped in front of her and took off his cap.

'What is it, Gregory?'

'*Proszę* Pani . . .' He was still breathless. 'Two Russians . . . they're by the river . . .'

'Russians? Soldiers?'

'Looks like town types . . . with their coats and that.'

'Well, what do they want, Gregory?'

'Want?' Gregory blinked. 'They don't want nothing.'

'I'll come and talk to them.'

'You can't!'

'Why not?'

'They're all tangled in the water and the reeds, and shot with holes in the body.'

'Dead?'

He nodded, shifting his weight from foot to foot.

Everyone had heard the rumours, the Russian rumours, the Bolshevik rumours. The border loomed in the east like the barbed-wire fringes of a forbidden world. Yet for some it was all just Polish propaganda, and they longed for the day when the barbed-wire would roll forward, crush Poland, and release them all from their frightful feudal yoke.

It was hard for these people to understand why so many tried to escape; why the few Russians who made it across the border told of famine, purges and the terrible silence that hung over the plains; and why those who hadn't made it floated down the Niemen with staring eyes and bullet holes puncturing their broadcloth coats.

'Somewhere about here,' Zofia was standing at the end of the Mantuski drive, 'I used to get this strange feeling. Like something approaching. Always here, by the cross.'

We looked carefully, but there was no sign of any cross.

In 1928 Adam and Bartek had selected this site to erect a wayside cross. Such things were a regular feature of village life and this place had always been a meeting-place, a place to idle, for wayfarers and ragpickers to rest and exchange news with the villagers. During the first war three partisans were hanged there, including one of Mantuski's gardeners, Michał.

The cross became known as Michał's Cross. Adam and Bartek had fashioned it from two beams of heavy oak. The beams were cut from an old tree which had to be felled to make way for Mantuski's byres.

'It was about six or seven feet high,' explained Zofia, raising one arm above her head. 'Dark, stained wood with dead flowers usually at the base. Goodness knows what became of it!'

We asked an old man wheeling a bicycle along the road. He appeared confused at first.

'Krzyż . . . krzyż . . .' He chewed on his gums and frowned. 'Krzyż . . . Oh yes! The *kolkhoz* committee took him down, took down the timber and the nails!'

He gazed at Zofia as if she were some exotic beast; he toyed with his *czapka*. Then he leaned forward and tapped her forearm: 'But I tell you them timbers were never right. They made a threshing machine from them and it broke a man's arm. No, it was never right, that machine . . .'

She asked him what happened to it.

'Burned!' The old man let out a high chuckle, threw up his arms and rode off in the direction of the river.

For the last few summers at Mantuski, Helena arranged for various young Englishmen to come and teach the children English.

Tony was the first, a quiet, methodical student-teacher whom they all took to at once. He led them through the tricky basics of English pronunciation, the long a's, the lisping th's. He made them read *Little Lord Fauntleroy*, whom Zofia thought a 'lovely little man'.

Zofia teased Tony mercilessly. He spoke not a word of Polish. Once, in a hotel bar in Lida, she had seen him raise his empty beer glass to the waitress, and say, 'Same again, please, Miss!'

After that Zofia chanted at every opportunity, 'Semagen plees mees!'

Tony spent a few hours with them each day, talking in his measured way, patiently correcting their mistakes and making a particular point of explaining the rules of grammar. He was a great one for rules.

The following year, 1938, he returned to Mantuski with a friend.

Eric appeared from the car ahead of Tony. He wore a cream linen jacket and baggy white flannels. He ran his eyes along the front of Mantuski, up to the trees, then let out a strange squeal of delight. Zofia watched him from her window; here, she thought, is a very different type of Englishman.

'He had a kind of magic about him. He was about nineteen at the time, always running about madly. Poland made him very wild. He said it took all the Englishness out of him. He would play constant tricks, lie in wait for the ghost, swim in

the Niemen at night and write long poems. We used to sit at
Philosophers' Corner discussing things for hours. Useless things!
I remember a long debate about where exactly a branch ends
and where the no-branch begins. That fascinated him . . . Dear
Eric!'

But there was a clash of attitudes between Eric and Helena,
and one incident that nearly saw him despatched back to
England.

Within a few days of arriving, he was found fighting on the
landing with Zofia and two of her cousins. They were all in
their pyjamas; Eric was still dressed. Helena took him aside the
following day. 'I will not tolerate this sort of behaviour. It is
scandalous! You are not in England now, and these are not
English girls!'

After that, Helena always considered Eric rather Godless.
But he and Zofia shared precisely the same spirit, the same
mischief and exuberance. After that first summer, they began
to write to each other – he in a slightly simplified English; she
in her own curious, half-tutored version:

> November 1938. Mantuski.
> Dear Eric,
> I think you dance all the time and ran on Piccadilly
> and strike the hats of policemen . . . You must come
> quickly to Poland, I am sure it will be a lovely
> summer and we shall speak about curious ideas and
> do exciting things . . . Do you remember how you
> jumped in the river and saved Murzynek? Now I
> began to laugh so much at it that the dogs look at
> me in amazement . . .
> I don't feel inspired to wright more curious things
> by letter, we shall speak of it when you come. You
> must wear a scarlet moustache (then afterwards you
> can shave it). And you must be responsible and

reserved (much, heeps more than you were). It will
be my business to learn you and I am good at it . . .
Are you still romantic and do you like still to suck
your fingers? We often think of you and speak of
you. We all think you are a honestly nice chap. We
went on a holiday. We were in mountains in the
south, suspended over enormous precipices. It was
very thrilling. We thought there will be the war. If
there was I would go to the army, so I was very
excited. In the end of this month I will have 17
years. Very old how this life is passing. Now, Faty,
don't be lazy and write. The dogs are saying hello. I
never know how to finish a letter to Englishman . . .

Helena was now ill much of the time. Since Adam's death
she had become diabetic, had constant colds, an up-and-down
temperature and increasing trouble with her joints. In March
1939, on the advice of her various doctors, she travelled across
Europe to take the waters at Montecatini.

She spent five weeks away. She was alone and, by her own
account, very happy. She was very happy after a week at the
spa, happy reading Charles Morgan's *Sparkenbroke*, happy in
Lucca among the narrow ochre streets and the cool stone
churches, happy in the leafy little squares, in Pisa, in the hotels
and trains, and happiest of all by the sea at Livorno. There she
spent a whole day watching the surf, before writing:

> The sun is setting. The lighthouses of Livorno and Viar-
> eggio are winking to the right and to the left. The bells
> of the monasteries are ringing for vespers. I pray that
> I may be allowed to return here and spend my last days
> here. I want to be near Adam but I do not, not really,
> want to be buried in that Broński vault. May I die by
> this sea.

She listed twelve 'admirers' during those weeks, twelve men drawn in by her solitude, twelve men left high and dry at her door. Professors, Frenchmen, a Swiss painter, came and went. Then there was the Italian count in Rome who had urged her to 'take life as it comes'. She had felt suddenly young and impulsive in his presence, drugged by his words.

'Look!' he had said, gesturing down on the rooftops of Rome from his villa. 'Look how beautiful the world is! How can you waste it all, Helena? How can you shut yourself away?'

But she had remembered that other Satanic hand offering the world, that other mountain, and she had woken from her trance and fled the Italian count.

The high blue of the Alps revived her, Munich was quiet, Berlin was horrifying. She could not believe the change in a few years. The city was 'hypnotized by Hitler', a picture of him in every window, brown shirts on every corner. At the border she was bustled and jostled by slim young giants with swastika arm-bands. They made all the Poles wait for hours. Arriving back at Mantuski, she recorded, was like coming out of a bad dream.

The following morning, early, she wandered through the forest. She walked out past Michał's Cross to the river and sat on the bank. She watched the first swallows weave through the still air. She was transported by the familiar ecstasy, the old ecstasy of the forest. The horrors of the new Europe fell from her.

'What human assembly', she wrote, 'can bring such peace? I adore watching the cool green river below. I love seeing the dear house through the trees, seeing the dogs at my feet. I love the absorbing work of this place; I love it all. I would rather perish here than leave.'

But she knew as soon as she had written it that it was not going to be so simple.

* * *

There was something strange about the spring of 1939. The thaw came late, and suddenly. One day the Niemen was frozen and the next it was bubbling out of Russia with a barbarous fury. In a matter of hours, acres of river-bank had been lost to the flood, peeled away from the bank like turfy icebergs.

Then in May the water dropped and remained pitifully low all summer.

The Mantuski stork, which every year had nested in a dead oak beyond the lawn, failed to return. And it was nearly June before the first nightingale was heard.

Helena sat by the window, listening to the news on the wireless. She kept her darker thoughts to herself. She gave the children leather belts and gold roubles to sew into them. She had been collecting the roubles over the years. They bore the head of Tsar Nicholas II; she knew that if the chaos came again, they would be the only currency of any use.

Zofia remembers sewing the rouble-belts that summer, but little of the sense of threat. To her the summer of 1939 seemed much like all the others – except that it was hotter, and that Eric was back.

He and Zofia renewed their enthusiasm for long and useless debates at Philosophers' Corner. Eric had brought a copy of *The Wasteland*. He read out long passages while Zofia sat watching the river.

'I hardly understood a word!' she told me. 'The English went way over my head. All I remember was "the moon shone bright on Mrs Porter / And on her daughter / They wash their feet in soda water"!'

(Many years later, Zofia met T. S. Eliot. She had translated his *Murder in the Cathedral* into Polish. In his preface to the edition, Eliot said he gathered it was a fine translation, though he himself did not have the Polish to judge. Zofia considered it a kind of revenge.)

Neither she nor Eric thought there would be war. They

talked about it at length, but Eric was a pacifist and convinced Zofia that France and Britain would, if it came to that, step in and scare Hitler away. But in late August, the threat suddenly closed in. Eric was rushed to catch the last plane out of Lithuania.

From then on, wrote Helena, a sort of unreal quality fell upon events.

26

ON 1 SEPTEMBER, at about eight a.m., Helena drew open the curtains of her room and counted twenty-four planes passing overhead. In the west, the Panzers rolled over the border into Poland. Within days the first refugees had arrived at Mantuski. They came with nothing but bundles of bedding and clothes, and fantastic stories of villages burnt, women taken, cattle crushed beneath the wheels of tanks, babies eaten.

It all happened so suddenly, no one had time to worry. Helena spent her time clearing the rooms and the farm buildings for the refugees. She relayed from the wireless reports of the Polish cavalry inflicting heavy losses on the Germans. But to her diaries she admitted the one question which haunted her: to stay at Mantuski, or to take her children to Wilno.

One afternoon, she went to see the Russian Woman. The two of them sat outside her cabin; three scraggy hens pecked in the dust around their feet.

'It's a bad time that's come again,' the Russian Woman said.

Helena nodded. There were occasions when even the Russian Woman's wisdom sounded trite.

'I'm thankful not to have children, Pani Helena. I have only my hens.' She scattered a handful of corn towards them. 'If anything happens I can eat them.'

There was silence for a moment. 'I have decided to leave,' Helena said.

The Russian Woman looked at her gravely. 'Give up your land now, Pani Helena, and you will always be lost, trying to rediscover it.'

'But, *ciocia*, how can I stay? Landowners will be murdered if they stay.'

The Russian Woman nodded sagely. A light wind rose from the south. It brushed through the birch leaves above their heads. 'It is like a curse to be born in this country, Pani Helena, a wretched curse . . .'

'And yet it's beautiful . . .'

'And God asks a heavy price when he bestows beauty. Dig down into this soil and you will find it bleeds – bleeds with the blood of Poles and Russians and French and Lord knows who else.'

The Russian Woman's wise words proved of little real help to Helena. Duty was the oracle she consulted next, and duty proved more lucid. Number one duty was to her children – they would go to Wilno, and from Wilno, if necessary, to the coast, to Norway, or England, or France. Number two was to her land, her household, her animals: she herself would return to Mantuski; she would remain at Mantuski like a captain with his ship.

Zofia said she felt it was dangerous to be split up. But her mother ignored her protests. She went off to Nowogródek to get passports, and to see Uncle Nicholas.

Zofia watched her leave, watched the black hood of the Ford fade behind a screen of dust. She then crossed to the stables and saddled Delilah. She would try and reach Uncle Nicholas before her mother; he alone had the influence to persuade her.

Zofia took the back route to Druków, through the forest; she did not want to meet her mother on the road. The trees closed in around her; the war seemed far away. She rode for two, three hours. Sprigs of hazel brushed at her hair. The forest was parched and tired after the hot summer. When the trees thinned, she slowed to a walk. Ahead appeared a long kidney-shaped field cropped of its rye. Beyond the field rose a forest of young spruce, and beyond them was Druków.

She skirted the field. From the forest came a noise – a breaking of twigs, a parting of leaves – and Delilah side-stepped into the stubble. Zofia watched the trees for a deer or a wild boar. But instead two men and a woman appeared. The men were carrying rifles.

'Who are you?' said the woman.

'I come from Mantuski – Zofia Brońska.'

'Why do you take this back route – why not the road?'

Zofia paused. 'I was lost.'

The woman looked at her closely. 'That is not the truth!'

The men ordered her to dismount. They searched her pockets and found nothing but a little bread and an apple. 'How do we know you are not a German paratrooper?'

'My uncle is Nicholas O'Breifne, from the *dwór* at Druków.'

'Take us to him.'

At Druków, Uncle Nicholas was ill. He came out of the house tying the cord of his dressing-gown. He blinked in the sunlight and barked at Zofia's captors, 'Of course she's my niece!'

Uncle Nicholas then listened to her concerns. 'Yes, Zosia. I will talk to your mother.' He then kissed her forehead and told her to hurry back to Mantuski. 'And take the main road this time!'

He was standing on the bottom step when she looked back, a portly figure in his silk dressing-gown waving with both hands. It was the last time she saw him.

Druków 1992. In the grounds of the O'Breifne chapel was a small mausoleum. The rain fell through the high beech trees and spilled onto the building's roof. From across the river came the sound of thunder.

We stood in the shelter of the mausoleum's portico – Zofia,

me, and a woman from the village. On the door, which was padlocked, was a small plaque which read: 'Count Nicholas O'Breifne 1862–1940'.

'The Russians came that morning,' the woman said. 'They shot the game-keeper and took the Count away on a hay-cart. I saw him lying in the back on some straw.'

The following spring, she said, he had returned. He could barely walk. Months in a Soviet jail had broken him and before long he died.

'So that's what became of him,' mused Zofia. 'That's what became of Uncle Nicholas.'

We stood there for a long time. The rain showed no sign of stopping; the village woman stared at it with the look of one who'd been staring at it for years.

In the end, for Helena, there was no choice to make, no trip to Wilno. Watching the progress of the Germans, listening to each news bulletin, she had pushed from her mind the other danger, the greater danger – from the east.

On 16 September, she had returned from Nowogródek quite late. The evening was still and quiet. She had walked with the dogs down by the Niemen and round by Michał's Cross. The sky was filled with the whine of planes but she was not unduly worried. Later she had found that she could not sleep, so took a small sleeping draught.

Her sleep was broken at five o'clock the following morning.

'Mama! Mama! The Russians!'

Helena opened her eyes and saw Zofia standing at her bed. 'Mama, they telephoned from the village! The Russians have invaded!'

Helena rose at once, stubbing her toe on the bed and cursing. She dressed in a new thick skirt and a green jacket which she had kept aside. (Buying them in Wilno, the thought had come to her suddenly: these are clothes to die in.) She gathered the household together to pray in the hall. Like her own mother in 1915, she read the '*Kto się w Opiekę*', 'Prayers to God's Providence':

> . . . *God will instruct His angels to attend*
> *Each of your movements*
> *And lead you, across the darkest place,*
> *The roughest place,*
> *Lest you bruise your foot against a stone* . . .

Outside, the sun cleared the tree-line. Stiletto shadows stretched across the fields. Beyond the Niemen, beyond the far bank, a mist seeped out of the forest. From the village came the sound of dogs and crowing cocks, and the herd lumbered out from milking, down the avenue towards the upper meadows.

Helena had no choice. Bartek said he would hide them all. He said that to risk the open roads was madness. But she knew it would be madness to stay: they would be betrayed in no time.

'We must go, Bartek.'

They had only a matter of hours. She went to her office. A silence had already settled there. She unhooked Adam's picture from the wall, and his service medal. From the safe she took two thousand zlotys in brand new notes, jewellery and a pistol. All these she put in a small leather bag. She went to the Klinika, unlocked the glass cabinet and took down a small bottle of arsenic. She then crossed the hall to the dining room.

There was a glass-fronted cupboard against one wall and its shelves were stacked with samovars, candelabras, a silver wolf, mustard pots, salt cellars. Taking two large mushroom baskets from the kitchen, Helena placed the silver inside and covered it with a scarf. She then found Zofia and they left by the back door to bury it in the new plantations.

Back at the house Bartek said the Russian forces were within eight miles of Mantuski. They were moving quickly.

Bartek had harnessed the two remaining horses. They waited beneath the larch. He had put blankets and food in the carts, and a rifle. For a moment everyone stood outside the house, the carts loaded and ready to leave. Bartek took off his *czapka*. Tessa shuffled from foot to foot. The others stood motionless. No one knew what to say.

Helena turned and climbed into the front cart. She motioned to Zofia to take the reins of the other. Still nothing was said. Bartek stepped forward and checked the harness of Helena's horse.

'Hurry!' he whispered.

Helena flicked the reins. She did not say goodbye. She knew it would not be long before she returned.

27

THEY CAME OUT OF the avenue, passed Michał's Cross and rode on through the village. Outside the church a number of people had gathered. They stood in formless groups, waiting. Some were leaning on scythes, others held their caps, folded like documents in their palms. Hearing the carts, they shuffled aside. They fell silent, and the horses trotted past them.

Helena could not bear to look; she could not bear to see their hatred – could bear even less the sight of those who did not hate her. Again she thought: I cannot leave, I will see the children are safe and then return.

They kept north of the Niemen. The roads were empty. A breathless heat lay on the land and the clouds were thick and thundery. The forests stood motionless beneath them. Out of the distance came the soft thud of shellfire.

Helena's plan was to reach Wilno. The Poles were there in great numbers. There she could wait while it became clear what was happening. But in the first village they reached, it was obvious this would not be possible: the road to Wilno was already blocked by the Russians.

They rode on to the *dwór* of a friend. Trotting out of the long avenue they found its windows shuttered, its front door locked, its stables empty.

They returned to the road and, while the horses rested, took shelter in an empty barn. Their options, Helena realized, were narrowing. It was at this point that she toyed with the bottle of poison in her pocket for the first time.

After some twenty minutes there came the rattle of another

cart and Helena peered through the crack of the barn-door. A priest, an elderly man, was driving a farm cart towards them. She stepped out of the barn to greet him. They eyed each other nervously.

'Father,' Helena nodded up at him.

'*Dzień dobry*,' mumbled the priest.

'Where are you from?'

'Lipniszki. You?'

'Mantuski.'

He looked at her more closely. 'You are Pani Brońska?'

She told him she was.

The priest said he had worked with Adam during the last war. 'A wonderful man!'

From inside his soutane, he took out a map. Dismounting, he spread it on the verge. He swept a bony hand across the routes and forests of Kresy.

Wilno was cut off to the north. The Russians were also advancing to the south. Russians lay to the east, Germans to the west. A narrow corridor, he explained, still ran north-west, between the fronts, one hundred and twenty miles to the Lithuanian frontier. How long the corridor would remain open they couldn't tell.

The priest said quietly. 'Either we give ourselves up, or –' He paused.

'Or what?'

'Or we put our trust in God and head for Lithuania.'

Helena needed no time to decide.

Yet both of them knew that Lithuania had already closed its borders.

Father Jarosław was a man of prophetic height. His limbs stretched with a strange elongated grace from his body and he moved them slowly. Helena found his presence a profound reassurance. Beside him on the cart sat the monstrance of his church.

It was early evening when they reached the edge of the next village. Seeing the priest, a woman invited them into her house, provided them with tea, bread and salt, vodka, and feed for the horses. She clutched the priest's hand. 'Pray for us all, Your Reverence; the Bolsheviks took my son the last time, took him and I never saw him since.'

The candles guttered suddenly and in the doorway stood the woman's husband. He was holding an old hunting-piece. 'Go!' he cried. 'Leave us alone! You will have us all slaughtered!'

They went. They drove on, back into the forest. They drove most of that evening. Sometimes there was a plane overhead and the sound of bombing. Towards dusk the air thickened and the storm came quickly, bringing a sudden wind that spun the sand into steeples on the road. The horses coughed and flicked up their heads. Then it began to rain.

'We must find shelter, Father!' shouted Helena. 'The horses cannot go on.'

Father Jarosław knew a blacksmith, a large and ruddy-faced man with a sheepskin waistcoat and a toothless smile. He lived in a forest cabin. He enveloped the priest in a great sheepskin hug and said he would do all he could to help.

'But I have to tell you,' he added, 'they've reached Lida, Father. It is only a matter of time.'

He had no stables, this blacksmith, so they covered the horses with furs, took out their bits, and unloaded piles of clover in front of them. The steam rose from their flanks as they ate.

Inside the blacksmith's house, two grimy-faced children sat at the hearth. One of them was jabbing a fork at a scavenging hen. Helena sat at a table with the priest who smiled in the half-light and told her he had 'seen the seal on their foreheads' that day: the seal that in the Book of Revelation marked the foreheads of those destined to survive when God let loose the furies upon the earth.

The rain fell heavily outside. It beat on the thatch and made a hissing sound on the bare earth beyond the door. Helena fell asleep. Her head rested on the table; the children lay on the floor. The priest and the blacksmith carried on a conversation whose muted tones lapped at the hinterland of her sleep.

It was still dark when Father Jarosław shook her shoulder. 'Quick, Pani Helena! There are tanks on the main road!'

She rose, still half asleep, and woke the children; she heard the deep growl in the distance, a noise that appeared to come up through the earth itself. Good God, she thought, we will never get through, and in her pocket she felt again for the bottle of poison.

It was still raining. They re-harnessed the horses and set off on a forest track behind the cottage. The noise of the tanks receded. All that day they rode through the forest. They rode circuitously, sometimes north, sometimes west, avoiding main roads and villages. But on occasions it was impossible and in the early afternoon they were forced onto a short stretch of road. After some time a car approached from the south, a black Chevrolet.

Helena grew anxious as it came closer. It drew to a halt beside them and through the window she saw the face of an elderly man, pasty-skinned, flustered with fear: it was her mother's first cousin, fleeing his estate near Lida. She urged him to take them with him.

He looked at her helplessly. His wife leaned across the bench seat. 'Hela, look! You can see we have no room!'

Her husband threw up his hands in despair. 'Useless! Useless! None of us will get out!' And he grated the car back into gear and drove away.

That evening Father Jarosław led them to a presbytery in a small, predominately Polish town. The priests had fled. The caretakers said that the Russians were still some way off, and moving now more north than west.

In the morning, Father Jarosław spread the map out on a large oak table in the hall. The Lithuanian border was still sixty miles away. They could not reach it before nightfall. They decided instead to head for a *dwór* named Antoków; there, they had heard, a number of Polish refugees had gathered.

They made steady progress. But the horses grew slower. They dragged their feet through the mud, nodding feebly as they struggled to pull the carts across the uneven ground. It was late afternoon when they reached a stream. The water was high from the rain. The beasts bowed their heads and drank and Helena bent to wash the sweat from their flanks.

When she looked up again, a group of four soldiers was standing in front of her on the track. Their rifles were raised. More men spilled out of the trees and an officer stepped out in front of them. They wore Polish uniforms.

Helena put a hand to her chest. 'Oh, thank God! I thought you were Russians!'

'You must give us your horses,' said the officer. 'The army needs your horses.'

'Take our horses, Major, and you will be leaving us for dead.'

She could see the man was afraid. 'Leave us the horses,' she said.

He stood aside and let them pass.

It was dark by the time they reached Antoków. There were many refugees, a good deal of them landowners. Everyone was asleep. Helena went to the kitchen to prepare food. Zofia found some coffee beans in their supplies. She poured water on the beans and heated up the mixture in the kitchen. She could not understand why it did not work. Nor could her mother. Neither of them had any idea how to make coffee.

'See how we'd starve if we had to live under the Bolsheviks, without servants!' laughed Helena.

The upstairs rooms of the house were scattered with sleeping refugees. The Brońskis found a corner in one and spread out their blankets. The room had no curtains and the moon fell on the sleeping forms as if on a line of hills. Helena stayed awake a long time. She tried to picture the Lithuanian frontier, the barrier lifting in front of her and the guards letting them all in. She couldn't. She gazed at the stars and prayed.

Soon after dawn, word reached the *dwór* that the Russians were closing in. Those who had cars set off for Wilno, which had still not fallen. The Mantuski carts were too slow for the convoy; Helena knew she must carry on for the border alone.

But there were one or two families who would not leave, who would not trust the open road, who felt a dignified surrender to the Russians was their best chance. Father Jarosław stayed with them. They stood awkwardly on the terrace as the Brońskis left, while Father Jarosław conducted prayers. They formed tight little family groups around him, hands clasped in front of them, straight and elegant in their breeches and ties, in their woollen skirts and lace collars, in all their condemned formality.

On the roads that morning there was more traffic, a bustle of carts and leaderless troops. The fighting was closer, the sound of shelling continuous. In one place some soldiers had gathered in a huddle on the side of the road, four of them, with one rifle between them.

Helena slowed as she passed. 'What is it?'

The soldiers turned to look up at her. They said nothing but drew back to let her see. The body of an officer lay twisted on the verge; he still clutched his service revolver where it pointed at his cheek, but his cheek was missing. Helena was frozen with shock: it was the major who, only the day before, had asked her for the horses.

She flicked her reins and rode on before the others had a chance to see.

They reached the frontier town of Orany soon afterwards. It

was little more than a stretched-out main street. A row of young linden trees had been planted along it. The town was in chaos. Soldiers and police ran backwards and forwards. From one of the few side-streets came the sound of rifle shots; scarves of smoke rose from its buildings; the still air shook with distant explosions. The Russians had not yet reached the town, but the fighting had begun.

They rode on. Beyond the town, the noise receded and they slowed to a walk. They were all exhausted. One of the horses on Zofia's cart had developed a sore on its shoulder where the shaft had rubbed; each step now the animal faltered.

The road dropped down steeply into a ravine. The Mareczanka river, which marked the frontier, ran along the bottom. They could see the bridge and the border post beyond it. A group of Lithuanian guards stood above the parapet. There was no one on the Polish side.

Helena stopped the carts. She took a couple of her Tsarist gold coins. In measured capitals she wrote a note:

URGENT – PLEASE SEND WIRE TO HRABINA
O'BREIFNE, KAUNAS:

'WAITING FRONTIER ORANY GREAT PERIL
ENTREAT
IMMEDIATE ADMISSION HELENA BRONSKA +
CHILDREN'

She left the carts and the children and crossed the bridge alone. She came out of the shade of the ravine and into the sun. As she walked, she could see beyond the guards to a small, busy settlement. Two or three oxen stood beneath a large oak tree, and villagers and soldiers milled around them.

Helena smiled to the guards as she approached. One of them flicked his gun at her, urging her back. She stood her ground. Out of the guardhouse came a bearded officer. A wedge of hair stuck up to one side of his head which he scratched noisily. He yawned.

'Please, Major, I have an urgent wire. Please send it.'

The officer looked at her, then smiled slowly. 'No.'

But she only half heard him. Over his shoulder, a man from the settlement had stopped on the edge of the bridge and was watching the scene – a young priest. Without thinking, Helena pushed past the guards. She could hear the soldiers shouting, the sound of their boots on the gravel. She reached the priest, pressed the note and the coins into his hand, and whispered: 'In the name of God, Father, send this wire!'

She felt the guards take her arms. She shrugged them off and turned, walking swiftly back ahead of them. 'Thank you, Major,' she said as she passed the officer.

She reached the others. No one said anything about the gunfire and shelling, which was getting closer all the time. They rode up out of the valley and back along the main road to a group of two or three wooden cottages. The place was choked with refugees. Three old men sat in the shade; one of them was picking at his boots, the others were staring at the trees. On the cottage benches, arranged outside, women sat peeling cabbages and plucking chickens.

Helena jumped down from her cart and spoke to one of the elderly men, a Pole.

'Can we wait here?' she asked.

'You have salt?'

She took down a large block of salt and said they had coffee too and brandy and some money . . .

'Money!' he scoffed. 'What use is money now?'

But he gestured to one of the buildings and there they found space to sleep. They went back outside to prepare food.

'What will happen now, Mama?' asked Zofia.

'Your grandmother will go to President Smetona.'

'And why should he do anything to help us?'

Helena smiled. 'When he was young the president had been a shepherd boy on her estate. She paid for his education and now he would do anything for her.'

But Helena herself was full of doubts.

That night, the shelling subsided. Word reached the refugees that a battle had been going on all day, near the railway line to the east, and now the Russians had won control of it. In the morning, everyone knew, they would be continuing the advance.

There was nothing they could do. Helena slept little. Around midnight, she left the cottage and went out to walk up and down the main road. A steady wind chased the clouds across the moon. There was a smell of apples in the air and also the dust of mushroom spores. Autumn had overcome the indolence of summer and Helena thought of Mantuski. She had always loved September's calm, the longer nights, the permitted sadness. Now she felt oddly robust. An inevitability had set in during the day. She had done all she could.

The morning began soon after six. Helena was asleep on the cottage floor when she heard the first shells falling on Orany. Tanks were approaching through the trees.

Helena rose quickly. 'One cart, Zosia, harness the two chestnuts. I will wake the others.'

On the road, the sound of fighting drew closer. The horses had about half a mile to go before the road dropped down towards the frontier. They could hear rifles now, and the voices of men in the trees. A group of Polish soldiers ran out suddenly in front of the cart, crossed the road, and dropped down into the ravine. Helena urged the horses into a canter.

Out of the trees came a unit of Russian troops. For a moment they appeared confused; they looked up and down the road. They saw the cart and opened fire. The bullets whined like hornets around it; one thudded into the side, splintering it. Then the road slewed down to the left and Helena did not look back. She saw the bridge, and the guardhouse beyond it and an armoured car. She drove for the bridge; if they shot at them, she thought, so be it. It was better than the Russians.

The officer waved frantically.

Beside him, his troops raised their rifles. Away up the ravine the Polish soldiers had regrouped on the edge of the river. A shell dropped into the water near them, and they hurried away downstream, around a bluff, out of sight.

'Madame Brońska!' The officer stepped in front of his troops.

She drove on towards the troops, but they did not fire. The officer waved to her and she drew level with him. 'Your cable,' he said. 'Your cable came through last night, from the President.'

The troops closed in behind the cart, and the Brońskis crossed into Lithuania.

'She was as brave as a lion! Goodness, when I think of it now, Mama's courage seems in-ceredible!'

In Belorussia, shortly after we had been to Mantuski, Zofia told me what she remembered of the escape. It was a much less detailed account than her mother's. She said that at the time she was 'too young and foolish' to be frightened. There was only one moment which really alarmed her.

They were driving through a village. It was late at night. They had no idea whether it was a friendly village or not, so they were cantering. Zofia was on her own in the last cart. She felt something tug at her reins and the horse slowed. She saw two or three men close in around her.

'I had a rifle and waved it at them. I shouted at the horses and shook the reins. Somehow we broke free.' She paused. 'But if there was one thing that really saved us, it was that Lipniszki priest. I wonder what happened to him.'

The next morning we went to Lipniszki. The church was set back a little from the main square. It had a high tower, and a compound with the leafy look of under-use. A cabin stood outside it, and on the verandah dozed an old man.

He woke as we approached and the white spade of his beard rose from his chest. 'Father Jarosław?' The old man nodded and led us back into the compound. Father Jarosław! He pointed to a neat well-kept grave near the fence.

The priest, it turned out, had also reached Lithuania. He had spent several years there. In 1944, during the German occupation, he returned to Lipniszki with the church's monstrance. He resumed his ministry. There was a typhus epidemic in the village and he had tirelessly visited the sick.

The old man's voice dropped to a whisper and he leaned towards us. 'But Father Jarosław got the typhus himself and the Lord took him.'

Zofia stood for a moment before his grave and crossed herself. Then she said, 'All these years I had wondered whether that priest wasn't some sort of angel, sent to guide us to safety.'

28

THE BROŃSKIS spent the rest of September in Lithuania,
then October, and half of November. They stayed with Helena's
mother at Platków.

After the dash to the border, the relief with which they
crossed it, the reality of their position began to sink in. Helena
wrote:

> So, the most feared and the most appalling thing hap-
> pened. We fled Mantuski, left our beloved Mantuski.
> The house rebuilt by Adam, the precious rooms, the
> carpets, the furniture and books – gone. Our beloved
> staff, the dogs, the herd carefully bred over seventeen
> years, the forest, the bees, the orchards, the dreaming
> river, all gone. We are homeless, beggarly, broken. No
> Poland. No Mantuski. Everything vanished like a *fata
> morgana*. And so many, so many left behind: Uncle
> Nicholas, the Stravinskis . . . I don't think I can write
> any more . . .

Zofia took long walks in the forest. Of that time she remembers the trees and an overwhelming sadness. She wrote to
Eric:

> We are living, but our moral forces are extinguished.
> Probably the Bolshevics will come here, so we try to
> go further. If I come to England, please help me to
> get some job. I can be a very good cook if I learn a
> bit because now we have nothing. I hope you are all

right. If we are not dead or made prisoners or so, I think I will see you in this life.

Goodbye Eric.

Three generations waited at Platków: Helena's mother, frail and timid in her old age; Helena herself, widowed, thirty-nine years old, hobbling with a stick on account of her knee; and Zofia in loose cotton dresses, long gypsy hair and pale blue eyes.

The Russians stopped at the Lithuanian border. They signed a pact with Smetona and the pressure eased for a while. But in November Helena made the decision to leave. Her mother urged her to stay, saying it would all be over soon and they could return to Mantuski. But Helena had been chased out once too often.

In late November, Zofia wrote to Eric; she told him they were trying to get to Britain:

> . . . Perhaps sometimes, if we don't drown in the sea, you will meet me on a London street, sad and hungry. I will say 'hallo Gugu' and you will say 'can I give you a penny for your bread?' And I will say, 'Oh no, I have lots of money.' Now goodbye, dear Eric. If I don't write for two months, that means I am no more in this world.

They reached Britain in December 1939, by way of Estonia, Stockholm and Oslo. In Bergen, there was a small coal ship bound for Newcastle. Eric met them at the docks. Zofia was struck by how formal he seemed. 'I learned then that an Englishman in England is very different from one in a Slavic country.'

The Broński family was dispersed, billeted on various families around the country. Zofia ended up at the Convent of the Holy Family of Nazareth in Enfield. She learnt to type, to take shorthand, perfected her English and was accepted to read English literature at Reading university.

She continued to see Eric. They referred frequently to those two summers at Mantuski. So much was changing; that alone seemed constant. Zofia wrote to him in May 1940:

> Enfield.
>   . . . streets streets and houses and chimneys and a sun so uncomfortable in all this town town town . . . I sit in the window and try to imagine. It is Mantuski – I walk in the marshes and the water makes a funny little noise at my feet and the song of the forest is all around. You are there too, Eryk, because I am not happy here now seeing the Enfield station and the old dirty houses and a brown train speeding past with a noise. And you are not happy either and you are going to the army and you can't be free any more – so let's imagine . . . Oh, it's all too real and annoying a life!

To begin with, during the phoney war, Eric had stuck to his pacifism. But when the fighting began in earnest, he joined up with the sudden zeal of a neophyte. At the end of 1941 he was sent to the Far East. He wrote to Zofia from the ship:

> . . . It is evening and everyone is leaning over the rails and dreamily watching the waves. We have been to two ports since I last wrote and there is so much to tell you I don't know where to start. You know, always moving, and stopping for a few days at these fairy-tale towns is marvellous and as you go on a kind of excited madness mounts and you feel the whole world is at your feet and that all the marvellous places you have ever heard of lie open to you . . . It was you who had much more imagination than I did. You always wanted to travel to the ends of the earth and I loved the forests of Poland and the Swiss moun-

tains and was content to stay near them. Dear Zosia, how you would love this now . . .

By early 1942, Eric was stationed in Singapore with an anti-tank unit. The Japanese had begun their offensive.

> Since the very beginning, strangely enough, I seem to have been involved in all the big engagements and lots of minor ones as well. Somehow I do not get frightened, because I have too much to do, but I don't feel a bit like Rupert Brooke. I don't believe in fate at all, but only in the blind Goddess of Chance.
>
> You know, Zosia, lately when I have been in action and often since, I keep on having sudden lovely glimpses of Mantuski. It is strange. Just for a moment I see the branches of the fir trees on the edge of the forest near the house, waving in the sunlight, but most of all the river, the sandbank and the sweep of the river opposite the village, and the river beside the meadows and the swirling of the surface and the noises of the water.
>
> Just then, there was a specially big burst of shell fire a few miles away and I wanted to weep as I wrote. I think it was the contrast. I must stop now. Goodbye, darling Zosia. I think you will find me more natural when I get back.
>
> With love. Eryk.

That was his last letter. At the time, Zofia was working in the Polish section of the BBC in London. Eric's sister telephoned her there. She told her what she knew: that Eric had been captured during the Japanese advance, that he had been imprisoned, that he had escaped with an American, that he was betrayed by some villagers, made to dig his own grave by the Japanese, and bayoneted into it.

* * *

I asked Zofia once if she would have married Eric.

'Pheelip, I really don't know. We talked of the future, of course, but we never made plans. Everything was happening so fast in those days. If I'd been sure about Eric, perhaps I would not have been able to marry so soon afterwards.'

A year after Eric's death, Zofia married a Spitfire pilot, a Pole. The wedding took place in the Catholic church in the Fulham Road. Helena was unable to come; she was ill with angina. The honeymoon was spent in Wales, in a lakeside hotel which granted free board to Polish airmen. Zofia remembers a series of fine autumn days and damp bracken. It was a brief spell of happiness stolen from the brown horror of the war. And it was a beginning.

After ten days, her husband had to go back to his squadron in Northolt; Zofia returned to London. They talked by telephone on the evenings he wasn't flying. A week after the honeymoon, he ran a mission into France. His Spitfire was returning home when it was shot down. They had been married less than three weeks. At the age of twenty-three, Zofia was a widow.

After the war she married an American diplomat. They settled in Cornwall and became hotel-keepers. They bought Braganza. Zofia ran the hotel cellars, wrote poems and sailed, badly, in *Memory*. She planted roses and escallonia hedges and camellia, and they had two children. But the pattern of loss continued. Their son was killed at twenty-one in a car crash. They went bankrupt and lost the hotels. Zofia's second husband died, quite naturally, at the age of eighty.

At Braganza there is a picture of her son, a pastel drawing. He is wearing a moustache. He had tried to brush his hair for the portrait, but you can see it made no difference: it was too wild and bushy to be properly controlled. He has Zofia's hooded eyes.

I saw that same face again, in St Petersburg. It was framed

in a small portrait in the Heroes Gallery of the Hermitage. Here, individually painted, are all the generals who helped push Napoleon back across the Niemen in 1812. Tsar Alexander I dominates the whole of one wall. His generals line the walls on either side. Half-way down on the left is one who, alone, is not looking at the portraitist. There is the same moustache, the same untameable hair.

Beneath the painting is written, in Cyrillic: General Graf I. O. O'Breifne.

One evening in 1992, several months after returning from Belorussia, Zofia and I were in her sitting room in Braganza. The picture of Mantuski hung above her head. It was dusk and the wind was rattling at the doors; a summer gale was on its way. Through the window, one of the trawlers was coming back into the bay. To one side of the window, the monkey-puzzle stood in the semi-darkness.

'Just here, about fifteen years ago,' said Zofia, 'I remember sitting with Mama. On the lawn the grandchildren – her great-grandchildren – were playing some noisy game. Not one of them spoke a word of Polish. English, French – but no Polish. None of her descendants had married a Pole. Mama was almost blind by then. She turned to me and said, quite matter-of-factly, "Sometimes I wonder whether I was right to bring you all out of Poland. Perhaps it would have been best just to have waited for the Russians."'

In exile, Helena settled in a corner of Surrey. There she shared a large mock-Tudor house with a female companion and various cats. It was an unremarkable house, in an unremarkable place. Except for one thing. In the pictures of it that Zofia showed me, it was surrounded by exactly the pine and birch woods which had surrounded Mantuski.

'As she got older, her eyesight failed. She became very demanding. Her own mother had died in Dublin just after the war. Being an O'Breifne – one of the Wild Geese, or at least the widow of one – made her a curiosity there. For Mama it was different. She lived here for more than forty years but never really settled. She was always trying to get me to go and live in Surrey, but how could I? I had my own family here. In the end she came here, in January 1981.

'She arrived wearing dark glasses and had a cat under her arm. I imagined she'd be here for years. But you know after only three weeks she had died. Dear Mama . . .'

Zofia looked out of the window. It was now almost dark. The trees were just a shadow against the bay beyond. Mist was spreading in from the west. From the lighthouse came the moan of the fog-horn.

Back in Mantuski, the larch was still standing. Pani Cichoń's house stood next to it. Twice, she had stepped in to stop the authorities cutting it down.

'Look,' she had pointed at the trunk, 'you can see the axe marks.'

Pani Cichoń had asked about the family, about Zofia's aunts and her brothers, and her mother and what had happened to them all. Suddenly she leaned forward, interrupting Zofia's reply. 'Yes, ten years ago the children were playing there and there was a thunderbolt. It came out of the sky and hit the tree! Hairs of the tree came spinning down' – Pani Cichoń made a spiralling motion in the air – 'it must have been then – it must have been the time Pani Helena died!'

Zofia plucked three of the green seed-cones from the tree. Back at Braganza, we tried to nurture them. We planted them in pots in the greenhouse, but nothing appeared in the pots except a couple of weeds. Only the following spring, with the pots half-forgotten on the floor of the greenhouse, did it become clear that the weeds were tiny larch shoots.

Epilogue

ZOFIA WENT BACK once more to Belorussia. It was June, a high blue Kresy June. The skies were cloudless, the air a matted buzz of insects. The chatter of finches filled the forests. In the hay-fields, teams of reapers swung their scythes with the eagerness of those who know that good days – like everything else – were in short supply.

It was two years since our first journey. Belorussia had dropped further into its particular well of post-Soviet torpor. Fistfuls of banknotes were needed for the tiniest purchase; the whole fabric of the towns was rotting. Disparities had grown, hostilities sharpened. A sense of stasis pervaded everything; only the forest seemed truly alive.

In Cornwall, in the meantime, Zofia had been raising money. She had opened an account, at the National Westminster Bank in Truro, and named it simply: 'Chapel'. Into this account went funds for the one thing she felt would bridge her two worlds, that would pay the debt of duty she felt towards her abandoned past: the restoration of the family chapel and the looted graves of her ancestors. House guests, friends and family had all chipped in; even her dentist had waived his fees for the cause when he heard that bodies had been dug up solely to recover gold teeth.

That April, down a crackling phone line, the Nowogródek priest had announced that work on the chapel was now almost complete. The opening ceremony would be on 30 June.

'Pheelip,' mused Zofia as we crossed the Belorussian border, 'supposing we get there and it is not finished. Supposing there is no roof. What do we do then?'

'It'll be ready,' I reassured her – though felt less than reassured myself. I poured two large measures from the bottle of expedition vodka. 'For crossing the border,' I said. 'Remember?'

Father Antoni Dziemianko, Polish Catholic priest of Nowogródek, was a man practised in dispelling doubt. I remembered him well from the last time. I remembered his didactic liturgies. I remembered his teak complexion, his large face, his large horizons. He had in the bad years spent several years as an underground priest, but now had come into his own. He alone in that dazed town had had energy; he alone managed to get things done.

That evening, with the final instalment of the Chapel Fund lodged in smuggled dollars in my pocket, we knocked on his door. He was writing up a sermon on an old Soviet typewriter. His sleeves were rolled up to the elbow. 'Pani Zofia! Pan Philip! *Proszę!*'

We sat down.

'Now, everything is ready for Thursday. A bus is leaving here at two o'clock. The village are killing a calf, and the bishop is coming from Grodno.'

'Oh, my goodness!' exclaimed Zofia. 'A bishop!'

Father Antoni rose and closed both doors. Sitting down at his desk, he unlocked a drawer and produced a small wooden box. Inside the box was a gold wedding ring and an oval locket. Behind the maculated glass of the locket, rested a tiny wisp of dark hair.

'The builders found them near the graves.'

I took the ring and squinted at the inscription on the inside: HB 4 VII 1842. 'Who would that be, Zosia?'

'I'm not sure. Some Broński or other . . .'

We handed over the dollars and took the small wooden box and its contents. Father Antoni saw us to the door. As we were leaving, Zofia turned. 'Oh, one more thing, Father. I wonder, could you ask the village to spare that poor calf?'

Outside it was dusk. The ruined castle of Nowogródek stood on the opposite hill like a shipwreck.

'What I can't understand,' said Zofia, 'is how the looters missed it. A wedding ring – I mean, wouldn't that be the first thing they would look for?'

'Perhaps it wasn't found by the builders at all.'

'What do you mean?'

'Perhaps someone in the village had a guilty conscience.'

The day of the ceremony had been chosen as a day of obligation, the Feast of St Peter and St Paul. By midday, it was very hot. A faint-hearted breeze did no more than tousle the fringe of the forest. Zofia and I arrived at the chapel early: she was to greet the bishop when he arrived, and present him with the keys. As we stepped up the path, a nun was laying a trail of blue lupins around the chapel door.

But the door was padlocked. A man went off to the village for the keys and returned, breathless. He shook his head. 'No key!' He began to force the lock with a crowbar.

'So,' I whispered to Zofia, 'that is what you must give to the bishop – a crowbar!'

The restoration, though, was magnificent. Outside, four robust columns supported a timber pediment; a simple black cross topped the pediment. One of the outer walls had been completely rebuilt – but so neatly that it was hard to tell which one. White-wash covered the columns and the walls and was so bright that Zofia had to dip into her handbag for a pair of sunglasses.

Inside the chapel, it smelt of new paint. Accustomed as we were in Belorussia to seeing ruins, it seemed odd to be looking at the fruits of fresh building. The interior was neat and modest. It was no more than forty feet long. A parquet floor stretched to a simple altar. All around the altar and the chapel were jars of lilies and peonies. The ceiling was made of stained larch, cut from the tree that had stood beside the ruins, and which two years earlier had guided us to the site.

Into one wall was set a granite tablet, and on it had been chiselled the inscription: Adam Broński 1890–1934. Zofia placed her bag on a chair and stood before the tablet. She stood there for several minutes.

Sixty years. Sixty years since her father's coffin had been carried into that chapel. Sixty years since the horse-drawn cortège had travelled through the forest from Mantuski. Sixty years. Sixty years in which all she'd thought was solid, all the people she'd loved, had vanished one by one. Here was where the parade of loss had begun.

We went outside. The heat rose from the stripped earth around the chapel. Zofia sat in the shade of one of the columns. Parties of villagers climbed the hill. They bore sheaves of flowers. They chattered in small groups, peering at the new elegance of the building, at the old elegance of Zofia. Slowly, they shuffled towards her, eyeing her clothes, her shoes, her sunglasses.

Proszę Pani, tell us, where is your home? Is this your son? Please tell us, where is the rest of the family? What has become of them all?

Canada, Anglia, Francja, Australia . . .

When will they come back? *Proszę* Pani, why are they not here?

It's far. Far, and many are poor. (How could she explain how difficult it was to return, how difficult it was to face what had happened?)

But they will come, *Proszę* Pani, won't they? Please tell them to come . . .

The Bishop of Grodno arrived at a few minutes before three. His German car slid to a halt. The crowd parted to let him through, and he smiled an episcopal smile and handed out plastic rosaries to the children. He entered the chapel, bowed, took his seat beside the altar, and placed a biretta on his head. There was no presentation of keys.

Six priests followed the bishop. Their suitcases of props – the mitre and crozier, the various liturgical soutanes, all the starched and glittering paraphernalia of the host, took up a sizeable part of the chapel. The people crammed in, packed the doorway; and those who could not fit – the majority – stood outside.

The service itself was a conventional Mass, with the addition of a reconsecration ceremony. This involved a series of prayers, and the bishop parading around the chapel with an aspergill, scattering holy water.

After Mass, Zofia stood to make a speech. She cleared her throat and looked at the faces before her.

'This chapel', she began, 'holds memorials to my family, the Brońskis. Once they all lived here and used this chapel for Mass, for their baptisms and weddings, and for their burials. I remember my father's funeral here sixty years ago – some of you told me you were here then too. That means an enormous amount to me. Thank you for coming.'

The crowd outside pressed in closer to hear; there was some jostling in the packed aisle.

She raised her head before continuing. 'Like you, my father lived all his life on this land. He loved the land more than anything else. He spent his life working it and when he wasn't working it, in the first war, he was fighting for it. He loved the people here and the forests and it is in his memory that this chapel has been restored.

'But there is one thing you must understand. For more than half a century now, no Broński has lived here. Once this was our home, but not any more. The family is scattered around the world and the life we knew here is gone. The restoration of the chapel is not for us; it is not for my family, but for you, for all of you – Belorussian and Pole, Orthodox and Catholic.

You must look after it as your own home. You must use it. Come here and pray whenever you want, whenever you can – even if there is no priest to officiate; you must say the rosary and in the spring cut back the forest around the building.

'And be warned,' she smiled, 'that if the chapel again falls into disrepair, it will be *my* ghost that comes back to haunt you!'

The next morning, Zofia rose late. We were staying with a Polish family, on the fourth floor of a crumbling block of flats in Nowogródek – six of us in three rooms.

'*Dzień dobry*, Pheelip. I feel rested,' she said.

'*Dzień dobry*, Zosia.' I kissed her cheek.

She sat down at the small table in the kitchen. 'Oh, I can't tell you what a tremendous relief I feel today!'

She had given me no idea how much she'd been dreading the whole thing – dreading the ceremony, dreading the speech, afraid that her Polish would fail her, or her legs, or that no one would come, or that those who did would be hostile.

'Yet you know, Pheelip,' she said, 'I honestly think that it was one of the best days of my life. Does that sound ridiculous?'

'No, Zosia, it does not.'

Before leaving Belorussia, there was one more thing we had to do. We drove to Mantuski.

Pani Wala Dobrałowicz, Zofia and Helena's one-time dressmaker, was feeding her bantams when we arrived, scattering seed on a patch of bare earth before her cabin. The bantams squawked at her feet. A single birch tree stood beyond her vegetable patch, its silvery leaves quivering in the wind. Beyond the birch was the Niemen.

When she saw us, Pani Wala let her pan of seed clatter to the ground. 'God, my God!' she cried, and came over, hugging us both as if we might fall apart.

Of all the people I met in the old region of Kresy, all the Poles

and Belorussians, the Lithuanians and Russians, the priests and
nuns, none left quite such a mark on me as Pani Wala. She
had eyes of the deepest cornflower blue and a pure and powerful
presence. But it was her speech that I remember best.

As she talked, you could sense a reservoir of feeling behind
her face; and sometimes the reservoir would spill over, filling
her eyes with tears, setting the corners of her mouth twitching.
The words would tumble out with the fluency of music. Then
pausing, she would laugh. The switch was miraculous; she was
the only person I have ever met who seemed utterly oblivious
to her own mood.

We followed her into her cabin, and sat while she bustled
around, shaking her head and muttering, before sitting down
with us.

'Only a little longer,' she sighed, looking up at the wedding
portrait on her wall. 'Just a little more of this and God will let
me join my Kazik.'

Her Kazik had died two years earlier. In the years before the
war, he had been the head gardener at Mantuski. He it was
who had tended the roses, trained the honeysuckle, and with
Helena each spring made the plans for planting.

We had lunch. Pani Wala laid out a clean white table-cloth;
she laid it with plates of potato and *kiełbasa* and herring. Zofia
presented her with a pair of shoes and two jerseys from Marks
& Spencer.

A bottle of vodka appeared. Normally, Pani Wala explained,
she never drank. 'But, Pani Zofia, I shall drink your coming!
I shall drink until I fall. I shall drink, drink, drink – three
times until I am completely out of knowledge! I shall drink for
you, Pani Zofia; I shall drink for you, Pan Pheelip. I shall drink
like an Englishwoman!'

And we did drink, and talked and ate and drank again, and
slept it off in the close heat of the afternoon – the two widows
on beds behind a screen, me on an old sofa next to the stove.

It was nearly four when I rose and tiptoed out of the cabin.

I walked out along the river. Its eddies twisted and slid past my feet. The wind pulled at the high grass on the bank. Down near the *dwór* were the ruins of the brick factory. The chimney still stood, the same chimney that had been there in Zofia's day, the same chimney that rose above the ruins when Helena arrived in 1920. Some hardboard huts had been erected beneath it, and inside them were signs of the new age, the age of 'beesnees' and kiosks: village girls were filling bottles marked Tutti Frutti Shampoo and Fleur Raspberry Bath Essence.

I carried on. Nearer the site of the old house, one of the limes of the avenue had fallen in the last year. The larch still dominated the skyline, though one or two of its boughs were bare with age. On the mound – all that remained of the old house – shards of red brick were still visible in the soil.

We spent the night in Pani Wala's cabin. Zofia wore a pair of white satin pyjamas. I could hear the two women talking behind their screen long into the night.

In the morning, shortly after dawn, I left the cabin. I went outside and sat beneath Pani Wala's birch tree. Zofia came out shortly afterwards, tying up the cord of her red silk dressing-gown. She walked into the vegetable plot. She stood there watching the Niemen, watching the mist rise from the water. All around her were calf-high potato plants, cabbages, sprigs of parsley and onions.

For several minutes nothing moved. Then from the pines there came a cackle of rooks. Zofia raised her head to listen. It was the same sound that started her days in Cornwall, that spilled out of the high chestnuts at Braganza.

She placed one hand casually against her throat. She remained there for some time, quite still, while her dressing-gown trailed like a bridal train through Pani Wala's sprouting onions.

*   *   *

We left Belorussia as we'd come in, on a beaten-up old bus. The whole chassis of the bus was skewed; a sunburst fracture filled the windscreen. The driver shrugged. 'Perestroika,' he said.

The bus had been chartered to take a party of schoolchildren on holiday to Poland. Their parents followed them on board, bringing with them bags and bags of old clothes and household goods to sell in Warsaw for 'ice cream money'. The bags made us feel like refugees.

We sat at the back, among the refugee bags. Zofia leaned against them, and said, 'Pheelip, what do you think? Will I ever come back here?'

'No.'

She looked out of the window, watching the buildings of Nowogródek give way to the fields and the forest. The sun was low on the horizon. 'No, I think you're right.'

Then she raised her chin and smiled her reckless half-smile. 'But maybe when I'm very old I'll come here in a car and stay in a little cabin in Mantuski and die there all alone!'

We reached the border at dusk. Queues of stationary buses stretched back down the road, like the vertebrae of some fossilized reptile.

There was an incident at the border, a small everyday incident. After seven hours of waiting, seven hours edging down the line, filling in forms, passing checkpoints, we cleared the Belorussian side. By then it was well after midnight. On the other side of no man's land, a Polish guard came on board. He was very different from his Belorussian counterparts. With high uhlan boots, a hay-maker's tan and a hero's blue eyes, he had all the swagger of the re-emerging Poland. He stepped down the aisle. He counted the children's sleeping heads, asked for the driver's papers, tapped them with a pencil and said no, you must go back into Belorussia, back to your own town.

Zofia told me later that she saw red; she felt her blood boil

— it was the look he gave 'that poor Belorussian driver'. She came hobbling down the aisle. She'd started shouting at the guard before she reached him: 'How dare you! Can't you see these are just children? Really, you make me ashamed. You make me ashamed to be Polish!'

I told her to keep quiet. Pragmatism had taught me two things at borders: 'no' does not always mean 'no', and never lose your temper, never argue principles.

But who was I to know? What use had pragmatism proved at that other border, fifty-five years earlier, with Russian bullets hissing around her head, with the world gone mad, with Poland dying at her feet?

The Polish guard left the bus. He took the papers with him. In the end he did let us through. Perhaps we were both right.

Beyond the frontier was another queue of cars. They were lit up briefly in our headlights. We passed the queue's end and carried on into the night. Everyone on the bus settled down to sleep. The driver lit a cigarette; soon the only sound was the growl of the engine. In the darkness, the ranks of birch trees slid past the window.

At the back of the bus, resting against the refugee bags, her legs stretched out over the broken seats, lay Zofia. Her eyes were closed and she was breathing evenly; her arms were wrapped tight around herself for warmth. Above her, one of the windows was open and the night breeze was coming through it, flicking at the curtain, and tugging at the tuft of grey hair that hung down over her face.

BACK IN LONDON, we went our separate ways. Zofia had her paying guests to look after, I had a book to finish. All that summer when I telephoned or we wrote, she seemed to be ill, beset by a series of minor complaints. In November when I returned to Cornwall she looked tired and said she was going to hospital for tests. Two days later they operated, and found her abdomen riddled with cancer.

She outlived the couple of months the doctors gave her to live. She recovered well from the operation and had treatment in the spring. She also kept an imaginary black knife, she told me, and in the still hours after dawn would steer it down towards the cancer and cut it away, cell by cell. One morning she rang, laughing with the laugh I knew hid some elemental fear. She said she had had a terrible nightmare – the Red Army had come to Braganza and thrown her on the rubbish heap; for some time after she woke, she lay there convinced she was back in Mantuski, back beside the Niemen – until she heard the sea breaking against the rocks below.

The summer was as normal – Braganza full of family and paying guests and dogs and everyone was amazed what a recovery she had made. But when I saw her again in September, there were moments on our own when the mask dropped and she seemed suddenly far away. And it was odd at that time that I did not feel any of the mad urgency I had been expecting, the sense that our time was running out. It was as though we both knew that we could never do anything more together than those long Cornish winters, the Belorussian journeys, the chapel, this book. And when I saw her for the last time, and she was in her high-backed chair with the sea beyond her full of sun, it is not what was said that I remember but the time after we'd talked and we sat in silence and did not need to say anything more.

In late October, on a grey afternoon, the season finished. Zofia waved goodbye to her last guest, closed the door of Braganza and went to bed. Four days later, she died.

DATE DUE

MAY 5 '95			
FE 22 '95			

Demco, Inc. 38-293